Fabulous Jewelry
from Found Objects

Fabulous Jewelry from Found Objects

Creative Projects, Simple Techniques

Marthe Le Van

LARK BOOKS

A Division of Sterling Publishing Co., Inc.
New York

ART DIRECTORS: Tom Metcalf (photography) • 828, Inc. (layout) • **COVER DESIGNER:** Barbara Zaretsky

ASSISTANT EDITOR: Nathalie Mornu • **ASSOCIATE ART DIRECTOR:** Shannon Yokeley • **EDITORIAL ASSISTANCE:** Delores Gosnell

EDITORIAL INTERNS: Matthew M. Paden, Amanda Wheeler • **PHOTOGRAPHER:** Steve Mann • **COVER PHOTOGRAPHER:** keithwright.com

ILLUSTRATOR: Orrin Lundgren • **PROOFREADER:** Kim Catanzarite

Library of Congress Cataloging-in-Publication Data

Le Van, Marthe.
  Fabulous jewelry from found objects : creative projects, simple techniques / Marthe Le Van.
      p. cm.
  Includes index.
  ISBN 1-57990-562-5 (hardcover)
  1. Jewelry making. 2. Found objects (Art) I. Title.
TT212.L49 2005
745.594'2--dc22

                            2004024301

10 9 8 7 6 5 4 3 2

Published by Lark Books, A Division of
Sterling Publishing Co., Inc.
387 Park Avenue South, New York, N.Y. 10016

© 2005, Lark Books

Distributed in Canada by Sterling Publishing,
c/o Canadian Manda Group, 165 Dufferin Street
Toronto, Ontario, Canada M6K 3H6

Distributed in the United Kingdom by GMC Distribution Services,
Castle Place, 166 High Street, Lewes, East Sussex, England BN7 1XU

Distributed in Australia by Capricorn Link (Australia) Pty Ltd.,
P.O. Box 704, Windsor, NSW 2756 Australia

If you have questions or comments about this book, please contact:
Lark Books
67 Broadway
Asheville, NC 28801
(828) 253-0467

Manufactured in China

ISBN 13: 978-1-57990-562-0
ISBN 10: 1-57990-562-5

For information about custom editions, special sales, premium and corporate purchases, please contact Sterling Special Sales Department at 800-805-5489 or specialsales@sterlingpub.com.

Cover: **JOANNA GOLLBERG**
Toothpick Necklace
Photo by Keith Wright

Back cover, top: **J. FRED WOELL**
Looking Back/U.S.A., M.M. #1
Photo by artist

Back cover, center: **MERRY RADTKE**
Driftwood Brooch
Photo by Steve Mann

Back cover, bottom: **RON PASCHO**
Bottle Cap Bracelets
Photo by Steve Mann

Front flap: **TERRY TAYLOR**
Tin Tastic Bangle
Photo by Steve Mann

Back flap: **JANE ANN WYNN**
Tintype Necklace
Photo by Steve Mann

Spine: **TERRY TAYLOR**
Bakelite Button Pin & Posts (detail)
Photo by Steve Mann

Title Page: **RON PASCHO**
Bottle Cap Bracelets, 2004
Bottle caps, brass, copper BBs, beads; fabricated, cold connected
Photo by Steve Mann

contents

introduction

as I trudge uphill to work every day, I practice an improvised form of urban archeology, scanning the sidewalk for interesting bits and pieces that cross my path. One day I might find a bicycle reflector, the next, a rusty washer and a sweet gum ball. A colored sunglass lens may catch my eye the same way a finely cut gem would. A scrap of electrical wire may sway me as much as precious metal. A blue jay feather. A wacky candy wrapper. The perfect stone. These are the snippets of our lives, which speak volumes about us as consumers and collectors, and can become valuable resources for making all types of art—altered books, collage, shrines, sculpture, and as featured here, jewelry.

Found object jewelers value the visual, tactile, and symbolic appeal of an object as much as its material worth, and that is why I have developed such a deep respect for, and interest in, this work. Found object jewelry can be shocking, humorous, poignant, and enlightening. At the same time, it can be well designed and stylish. The more than 40 projects and nearly 100 gallery images in this book demonstrate that working with found objects is an innovative and inspiring avenue of jewelry making.

Whether you're an experienced jeweler or completely new to the craft, this book will strengthen your skills, open your mind, and spark your imagination. The Basics chapter begins with an overview of the materials and tools needed for metalworking. It continues with a survey of basic techniques and construction methods for making metal jewelry. Though the projects focus on found objects, you'll still need a working knowledge of such skills as sawing, piercing, forming, riveting, and soldering metal.

Finally, The Basics includes many special methods for working with found objects. Here you'll find ways to identify and preserve found metal; drill glass, ceramic, and stone; and cut and polish plastics. You'll also find a glossary of the commercial findings that can help you integrate found objects into your jewelry designs.

Sixteen artists designed the found object pieces that appear in The Projects section. The stylistic diversity is astounding and the level of complexity is broad. From simple sewing and stringing projects to more advanced ones that involve soldering and setting, there is an incredible variety from which to choose. If you have a fondness for jewelry that has an earthy look, give Jason Janow's *River Stone Pin* or Rachel Dow's *Seashell Parure* a try. Bric-a-brac fanatics can find fabulous reasons to plunder their collections when making the *Lost Earring Bib* by Brenda Sue Lansdowne or the *Sew Fine Brooch* by Lilla Le Vine. Mary Hettmansperger's *Hardware Charm Bracelet* and Elizabeth A. Hake's *Knotted Rubber Bracelet* have an urban industrial appeal and make great use of recycled materials. Looking for an unforgettable way to accessorize a party dress? Search no further than Joanna Gollberg's *Toothpick Necklace* or Susan Lenart Kazmer's *Energy Talisman*. In both of these projects, the simple repetition of form results in jewelry of uncommon beauty.

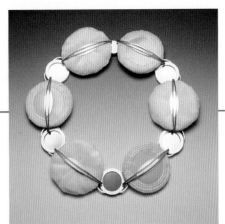

Attractive photography and easy-to-follow instructions accompany each project. You can closely adhere to the directions, modify them for use with a particular found object, or use them as a starting point for your own creation. Some projects, such as Terry Taylor's *Show-Me-the-Money Bangles & Dangles*, are made with a very specific type of found metal, in this case salvaged symbols from an antique pricing display. Realizing that this exact material would be difficult, if not impossible, for you to find, the designer has offered a variation on his project made with recycled food tins. Occasionally, such substitutions are not only necessary but welcome, as you explore the infinite possibilities of using found objects.

Insightful quotes from many of the project artists are included, giving the creators a chance to express their attraction to specific materials and describe their motivation and creative process. Two additional special features run throughout this section: Check It Out contains interesting facts about found objects, and Track It Down provides tips for locating materials.

Fifty internationally recognized artists are represented in the gallery. Spread throughout the book are jewelry pieces ranging from minimalist compositions to spontaneous and quirky assemblages. Jennifer Trask's exquisitely elegant *Popillia Japonica* brooch uses Japanese beetles like gemstones. By contrasting found iron with 22-karat gold, Emanuela Zaietta's *Sun* ring is quiet but profound. Kristin Mitsu Shiga and Aaron Mascai pay tribute to the natural world, while Harriete Estel Berman and Ron Pascho focus their talents on reclaiming and refashioning post-consumer waste. Biting social satire can be found in works as different as Tara Stephenson's *Select Cover Up* and Ken Thibado's *Concern*.

Those seeking enlightenment often practice conscious living. To those seeking to create jewelry from found objects, I recommend a practice of conscious *looking*. Aesthetically engaging materials are all around you. All it takes on your part is active observation. As you're taking out the recycling, cleaning out the garage, working in the garden, or strolling down

the sidewalk, keep your eyes open for anything that grabs your attention. When something does, trust your instincts and save that item. Something about its shape, color, or texture was immediately appealing and it had value to you. Chances are, you can find a fabulous use for it in an exceptional piece of jewelry.

materials, tools & supplies

Found objects come in infinite forms. Rather than attempting to cover the unique characteristics of each, this chapter focuses on the materials you'll need to fabricate jewelry from them. The tools and supplies described are those used for both the most simple and most complex projects in this book.

EMANUELA ZAIETTA
Sun, 2003
1⅝ in. (4 cm) in diameter
Found iron, 22-karat gold;
constructed
Photo by artist

Metal

Many found object jewelry pieces include salvage metal. These unique materials are usually recycled and repurposed post-consumer waste. They may be instantly recognizable or they may have developed a distinctive patina over time. It will often be necessary, however, to use sheets, wires, or tubes of new metal to turn your found treasures into jewelry. Here are some properties and characteristics of the most common types.

Metal Types

Metals are classified into two groups, ferrous and nonferrous. Ferrous metals either are iron or contain iron while nonferrous metals have no iron content. Nonferrous metals are most frequently used to make jewelry, although some wonderful work can be created from ferrous metals.

SILVER

A beautiful and durable material, sterling silver is basically the standard silver used in jewelry today.

Found metal, ferrous and nonferrous

Sheet metal in copper, silver, and gold

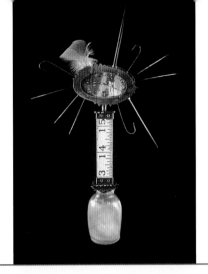

Left:
NISA BLACKMON
Talisman for the Looking-Glass Self, 1996
9 x 5 x 1 in. (22.9 x 12.7 x 2.5 cm)
Copper, red brass, mirror, ruler,
photo, cactus spines, porcupine quills,
fish hooks, parrot feather, glass;
fabricated, riveted
Photo by artist

Right:
J. FRED WOELL
Looking Back/U.S.A., M.M. #1, 2004
1 x 2⅝ in. (2.5 x 6.7 cm) in diameter
Aluminum, steel, paper, brass
Photo by artist

Contrary to popular belief, sterling silver isn't pure silver. Pure silver, commonly called fine silver, is a fairly soft metal. To boost pure silver's strength, it's made into an alloy. The most common metal with which silver is combined is copper. The composition of sterling silver is 92.5 percent silver and 7.5 percent copper.

GOLD

Like pure silver, pure gold is much too soft, and therefore impractical, for most jewelry making so it's usually mixed with other metals to make it more stable and more versatile. The measuring scale in the United States for indicating the purity of gold is the karat, and the higher the percentage of pure gold the higher the karat. Metals that are mixed with pure gold for strength can also change the color of the gold, resulting in different shades of yellow, white, pink, and even red and green gold.

PERCENTAGE OF PURE GOLD	U.S. MEASUREMENT	EUROPEAN MEASUREMENT
100	24 karat	999
75	18 karat	750
58.3	14 karat	585
41.6	10 karat	417

COPPER

Copper is a pure metal that works well for both cold and hot jewelry-making techniques. Initially bright reddish brown in color, copper can also acquire rich green and brick red patinas through chemical or heat treatments. Copper is highly malleable, making it easy to work, and low in cost, making it a popular metal, especially for beginning jewelers.

ALUMINUM

Like copper, aluminum is a pure nonferrous metal. Naturally good-looking, with a highly reflective grayish white color, aluminum is also lightweight (about one third as heavy as copper or steel). It's also eminently recyclable and ripe for repurposing. Soft and malleable, aluminum is extremely easy to form, machine, and cast. Anodized aluminum is coated with a protective or decorative film and sold in a range of brilliant colors.

NICOLE JACQUARD
Spring-Shadow Box Pendants, 2000
2 x ½ x 1½ in (5 x 1.3 x 3.6 cm)
Silver, 22-karat gold, butterfly wing,
glass, pearl
Photo by Kevin Montague

BRASS

Brass is an alloy of copper and zinc that has been used and prized since ancient times for its golden hue, hardness, and workability. Color variations of brass are the result of slightly different proportions of copper and zinc. It's more brittle than copper, harder to cut, and requires heating, also known as annealing, to stay soft during repeated hammering.

STEEL

Steel is the common name for a large family of iron alloys commonly made from iron ore, coal, and limestone. There are currently more than 3,500 different grades of steel with many different physical and chemical properties. Standard steels are classified into three major groups based on their chemical compositions: carbon steels, alloy steels, and stainless steels. Stainless steel is a broad term for a group of corrosion-resistant steels that contain chromium. Stainless doesn't mean these alloys will never stain or corrode, but they will stain less than steels that don't contain chromium.

OTHER METALS

There are many other interesting metals with which you can experiment. Some of these may have just the aesthetic or physical characteristics you seek for a found-object project. Among the easiest to find are bronze (an alloy of copper and tin and sometimes other elements), nickel silver, niobium, pewter, and titanium.

Metal Forms

Although some metalsmiths fabricate their own stock, most of the forms you need are readily available from jewelry and metal suppliers. I encourage you to order a catalog from one or more sources and browse their enormous selection.

Above: tubing in various shapes, sizes, and metals

Below: wire in various gauges

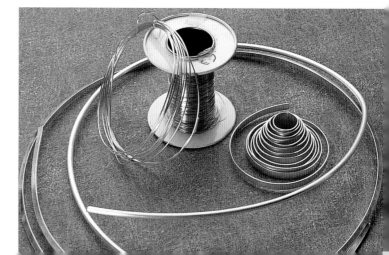

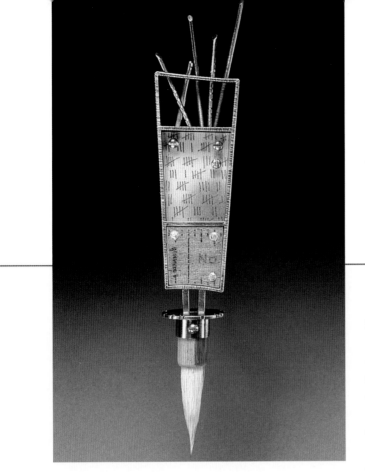

SHEET METAL

Flat sheets of both precious and base metals are manufactured and sold in different sizes. The thickness of the metal is referred to as its gauge. Gauge numbers inversely specify the thickness of the metal—the thinner the metal, the higher its gauge number. (For further information, see the standard gauge measurement chart on page 156.) From one manufacturer to the next, the same gauge sheet may slightly vary in thickness, but it should never be enough to affect the results of your jewelry. In addition to the ordinary square and rectangular sheets, metal suppliers also sell many precut flat shapes such as circles and triangles, and even more intricate designs, such as stars, leaves, and animals.

WIRE, ROD & TUBING

Metal wire is manufactured with many different profiles and in many different thicknesses. Round wire is the most common shape, but there is also half round, square, triangular, and more. Like sheet metal, the thickness of wire is measured using the gauge system. Precious metal wires are cut to the length ordered and priced by weight. Because they are less expensive, base metal wires are generally sold in predetermined lengths on a spool or in a coil. Metal rod is similar to wire in most ways, but rod is measured incrementally in millimeters rather than gauge and is available in larger sizes.

Tubing is a hollow metal cylinder. It's manufactured and sold with different wall thicknesses and diameters. Both of these measurements are given in millimeters rather than gauge. A tube has two diameters. One is measured outside the tube wall (the outside diameter, or OD) and one is measured inside the tube wall (the inside diameter, or ID).

Tools & Supplies for Metal

You don't need to run out and buy a bunch of new tools to begin making jewelry. Try a few simple projects first and gradually add new tools as your interest grows and your undertakings advance.

Jeweler's Bench & Bench Pin

A jeweler's bench is a wooden workstation specifically designed to meet the needs of metalsmiths. It has features such as tool drawers, catch trays, and precut holes to hold bench pins and mandrels. It is also built at the right height for healthy metalworking. (Bending over or reaching up for extended amounts of time can take a toll on the body!) Because a jeweler's bench is a well-crafted piece of furniture, it is a

DIANE A. ARCHER
Connected, 1997
34½ x ½ in. (87.6 x 1.3 cm)
Photoetched topographical map,
copper, glass vials, plants, soil,
animal teeth, animal bones, water,
human skin, human fingernails
Photo by artist

major investment. However, a sturdy wooden table
with an attachable clamp to hold a bench pin is a
perfectly acceptable setup if you're just starting out.
A standard wooden bench pin is used to support
metal for sawing, filing, etc. Most pins have a
V-shaped slot cut in at least one side.

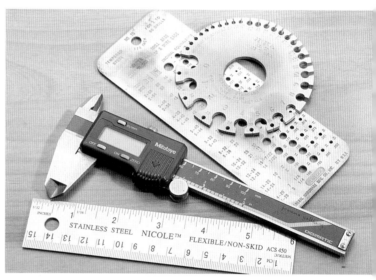

*Measuring tools, from bottom: stainless steel ruler, digital calipers,
drill bit gauge, wire gauge*

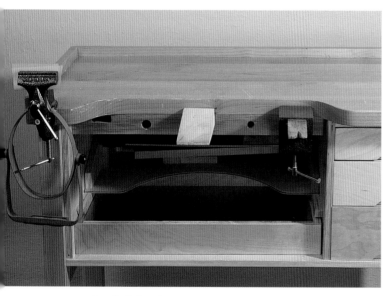

Jeweler's bench

Measuring & Drawing Tools

Jewelers who incorporate found objects into their art
still need to measure and mark their materials. Here
are some simple tools to make any project easier.

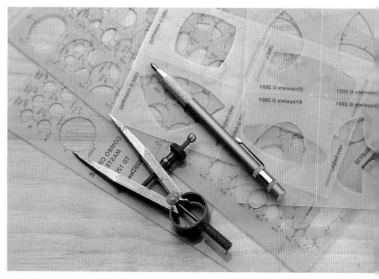

Marking tools, from left: templates, compass, scribe

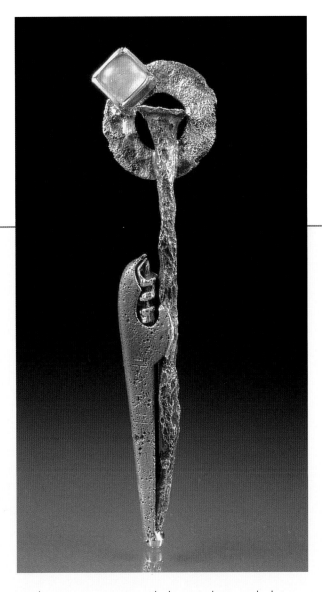

ROB JACKSON
Palio, 2001
3 x ⅞ x ⅜ in. (7.6 x 2.2 x 1 cm)
Antique iron nail, steel, 18-karat
gold, 20-karat gold, labradorite
Photo by artist

SCRIBE

A scribe is a pointed tool used to make marks on metal. You'll use a scribe to draw points and lines or to transfer designs. Make your own scribe by sharpening the end of a piece of scrap metal (such as a nail) or you can purchase a commercial scribe.

STAINLESS STEEL RULER

The precision and durability of a short stainless steel ruler is invaluable to any jeweler. This compact measuring device is easy to maneuver on small surfaces and resists damage well. Its lengths are given in small, easily divisible metric increments, such as centimeters and millimeters.

SEPARATORS, CALIPERS & TEMPLATES

Separators make measuring equal distances simple and precise. Simply set the two metal arms apart at the desired space, lock in this length, and measure the metal.

Calipers are used chiefly to measure thickness (gauge) or diameter of sheet metal, wire, rod, or tubing. Each pair usually has two adjustable jaws. Calipers are either digital, with an LCD screen, or analog, with a dial. Digital calipers are much more accurate, but much more expensive.

Having a selection of design templates is helpful for scribing common shapes onto metal. The templates can be plastic or metal with various sizes of cutout circles, ovals, squares, triangles, and more. If you need an instrument for measuring angles, a protractor can help you draw and plot your design.

Cutting & Smoothing Tools

Whether you need to trim sterling silver or soda cans, one of these tools will do the job. Once a piece is cut, make sure you smooth all sharp edges with files or sandpaper.

SHEARS, SNIPS & CLIPPERS

There are several ways to cut metal without using a jeweler's saw. With handheld metal shears, you can cut straight or curved lines in metal sheet. Shears with smaller blades allow you to cut more intricate

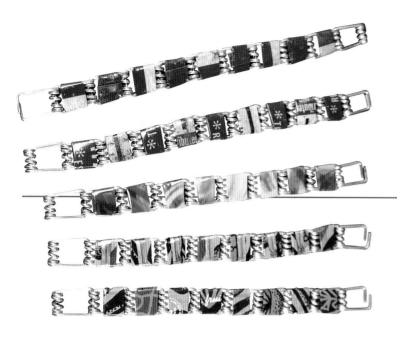

BRYAN S. PETERSEN
Clothespin Bracelets, 2002
½ x 6 x ¼ in. (1.3 x 15.2 x 0.6 cm)
Clothespin springs, tin; pattern
folded, assembled
Photo by artist

contours and patterns. Larger, table-mounted shears are also available. Snips, also known as cutters, are made for cutting wire. They have either flush or angled blades. Large-size nail clippers are also handy for cutting some types of wire.

Metal shears: curved blade (top), straight blade (bottom)

SAW FRAME & SAW BLADES

A high-quality, well-balanced jeweler's saw is one of the most important tools you can buy for metal-working. The open frame is made of rigid steel and can be adjusted for blade length and tension. The saw grip should be comfortable to hold. The throat depth of a jeweler's saw is the distance from the blade to the opposite vertical frame element. On standard frames, the throat depth ranges from 2¼ to 6 inches (5.7 to 15.2 cm). There are also jeweler's saws made with very deep frames for working on oversize projects. The throat depth of these frames is about 11 inches (27.9 cm). Jeweler's saw blades must be periodically replaced as they become dull or break. The saw frame is engineered to make this switch as easy as possible, using setscrews or clamps to hold the blade in place.

Saw blades are made from steel and steel alloys, and are manufactured in different sizes, 1/0, 2/0, and 3/0 being the most popular. Each brand of blade has a different thickness, depth, and teeth per 1 inch (2.5 cm). (Most jeweler's supply catalogs provide this information along with the correct size blade for each metal gauge and the drill size required for piercing.) Good saw blades have straight, uniform teeth and are flexible. Though they are more expensive, high-quality saw blades resist breakage and last longer, usually until they become dull. Low-end saw blades frequently snap or break, especially when used by beginners.

The more sawing experience you gain, the longer your blades will last.

Some specialty saw blades have unusual shapes and teeth configurations in order to cut materials other than metal. For example, blades that cut wax, rubber, plastic, shell, and other nontraditional materials have teeth that spiral up the handle. Stone, glass, and other materials can be cut with blades to which diamond particles have been affixed.

METAL FILES

Whether you use them to smooth the edge of sawed sheet metal or the edge of a found piece of scrap, metal files are important jewelry-making tools. They are constructed from a strong, tool-steel alloy and, with proper care, they should last a long time. "Hand file" is a broad term that describes all manual files used to remove, shape, or finish metal. These are generally 8 inches (20.3 cm) in total length with a cutting distance of 6 inches (15.2 cm). A hand file's "cut" size can range from very coarse to very fine. For removing metal quickly, start with the coarsest file, then switch to medium "cuts," and finally the finest file. Hand files also come with many different profiles, the most popular being flat, barrette, half round, and square. Many more contours are offered so you can more closely match the shape of the file to the shape of your metalwork.

Needle files are shorter, usually only 6 inches (15.2 cm) in total length, and much more narrow than hand files. Equally important to metalworking, needle files have a fine cut that is perfect for finishing and smoothing small metal elements, and their thin shape makes it easy to reach into tight areas. They are also offered in varied cut sizes and contours. Needle files

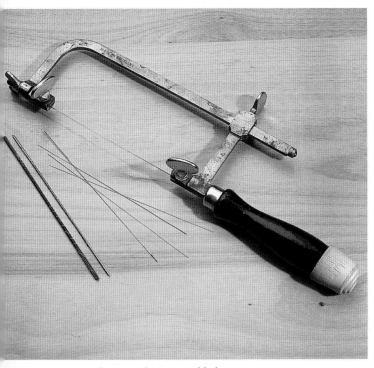

Jeweler's saw frame, saw blades

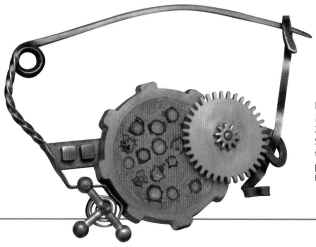

RON PASCHO
Fibula, 2003
3 x 2 x ½ in. (7.6 x 5.1 x 1.3 cm)
Sterling silver, clock gears, spring, toy
top, electrical conduit, colored concrete,
peppercorns; fabricated, riveted
Photo by Doug Yaple

are available with diamond particles attached. Use diamond files to contour and shape ceramic and glass as well as metal.

Assorted hand files

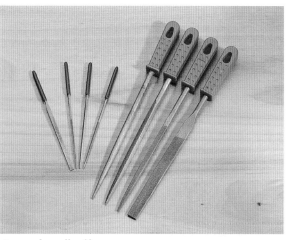

Assorted needles files

Hammering & Forming Tools

"Moving" metal is a significant part of the jeweler's art, and there are many ways to do it. Hammers are particularly useful when forming flat sheet, while different pliers facilitate and simplify wirework.

CHASING HAMMER

Specifically designed and weighted for metalworking, the head of a chasing hammer is made of polished steel and has two faces with different shapes. One face is wide, smooth, and slightly convex. Use it for striking other tools or planishing. The opposite end is ball-shaped. Use it for riveting and peening.

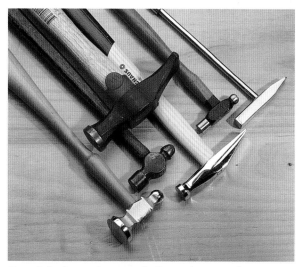

From left: chasing hammer, ball-peen hammer, forging hammer, goldsmith's hammer, small ball-peen hammer, riveting hammer

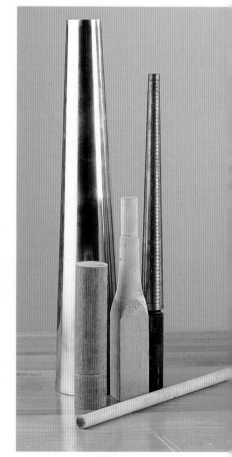

WENDY McALLISTER
Sea Music Brooch, 2001
1¾ x 3 x ½ in. (4.4 x 7.6 x 1.3 cm)
18-karat gold, sterling silver, wood
fragment from antique organ, coral;
hand fabricated
Photo by Norman Watkins

MALLETS

Wooden, rawhide, or rubber mallets are exceptional tools for forming, bending, and flattening metal. Large hammers with wide cylindrical heads and two flat faces, their greatest advantage is that they move metal without marring, scratching, or damaging its surface. Although less common, plastic and nylon mallets can perform the same functions as wooden or rawhide ones.

From left: mallet, steel block, daps, dapping block

STEEL BLOCK

Whether you're working at a jeweler's bench or on a worktable, it's most effective to hammer and form metal on top of a rigid steel block. The best bench blocks are made from tool steel that has been ground flat and polished. You can purchase one from a jeweler's supply store or make your own. Most blocks range from 2½ to 5 inches (6.4 cm to 12.7 cm) square.

MANDRELS

A mandrel is any type of sturdy form around which you can shape, straighten, or size metal. Commercial ring, bracelet, and necklace mandrels are made of metal or wood. Ring mandrels are tapered and marked with standard ring sizes. Bracelet mandrels have a gradual taper without markings, and necklace mandrels are designed to show how a piece will drape on the neck. You can hammer metal directly on or around most commercial mandrels. Feel free to use common household items as mandrels. Dowels and rods, even pencils, knitting needles, chopsticks, and rolling pins can be practical stand-ins.

From left: bracelet mandrel, various wooden mandrels, ring mandrel

ABRASHA
Royal Pachinko Ball Bracelet, 1993
4 in. (10.2 cm) in diameter
Stainless steel, 18-karat gold,
24-karat gold, steel pachinko balls;
fabricated, cold connected, riveted
Photo by Ronnie Tsai

PLIERS

Jeweler's pliers come in many different forms, most of them easily identifiable by their jaw shape. Round-nose pliers have fully rounded jaws that taper up from the base. Use them for looping wire, making jump rings, and bending wire and sheet. Chain-nose pliers are round on the outside of the jaw but flat on the inside, tapering up to a point. Use them for bending wire and sheet. Flat-nose pliers have flat and flush interior surfaces. The outside surfaces of their jaws are flat and angled. Use them to grip metal as you work and to create angular bends. Round-nose, chain-nose, and flat-nose pliers are commonly made of stainless steel or tool steel and are available in short and long jaw lengths. Although these three types of pliers will handle most jobs, there are many other specialty pliers that are worth investigating.

Clockwise, from left: combination-tip pliers, needle-nose pliers, flat-nose pliers, chain-nose pliers, parallel pliers

Drilling Tools

To pierce, rivet, or string jewelry components, you may have to create a hole or holes through them. Although it may seem difficult at first, drilling is a simple process that becomes easier with practice.

CENTER PUNCH

A center punch is a tool with one pointed end used to make a small dent on a metal surface prior to drilling. Standard center punches have one flat end that must be tapped with a hammer to make an indention. Automatic punches have an adjustable internal hammer that releases when the punch is pressed down on the metal. You can use a nail as a center punch if you sharpen its tip.

Center punch (left), automatic center punch (right)

JAN YAGER
Bullet Worry Strand, 1995–1999
18 inches (45.7 cm) from tip of
knife to top of loop
Found spent bullet casings,
knife, key, metal heart
Photo by Jack Ramsdale

DRILL BITS

Metal drill bits for jewelry making are much smaller than average drill bits. The chuck in the flexible shaft machine is specially sized to accommodate these smaller attachments. Most bits are made from hard and polished steel and can sustain the high speeds of the flex shaft. Most bits are measured by their diameter in millimeters, but some are manufactured and labeled to correspond with wire gauge sizes.

FLEXIBLE SHAFT MACHINE

A flexible shaft machine, or flex shaft, consists of a motor and a hand piece to which many devices, such as drill bits, burrs, cutters, and sanding disks, can be attached. Most flexible shaft machines are run by foot pedals, allowing you to control the speed of the motor. A long, flexible shaft connects the motor to the hand piece. It is important to keep a wide arch in the shaft so the machine will run safely and efficiently. A narrow arch or crimp near the motor or hand piece can cause premature wear and excess heat. To this end, it's advantageous to mount the motor of the flex shaft on a stand above your worktable or bench.

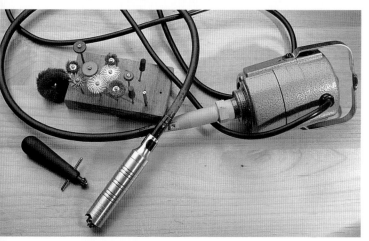

Flexible shaft machine and accessories

Jeweler's drill bits (left), diamond bits (right)

JUDITH HOYT
Grey Face Orange Mouth, 2003
Pendant, 4 x 2½ in. (10.2 x 6.4 cm)
Found metal, copper, steel; riveted
Photo by John Lenz

Cold Connection Tools & Materials

Found objects are frequently incorporated into jewelry with cold connections. Three of the most common ways to join or attach components are with rivets, settings, and adhesives.

FLARING TOOL

A flaring tool stretches open, or flares, the ends of tube rivets. These metal tools are available commercially or can be homemade from any number of materials as long as one end is tapered and one is flat for hammering. A worn out flexible shaft attachment or an old chasing tool makes a fine flaring tool.

BURNISHER

A burnisher is a versatile metalworking hand tool. Use it to gently shape and smooth metals, to open or close bezel settings, to even out surface imperfections, and to polish hard-to-reach places. Standard burnishers have wooden handles for a comfortable grip. The working end may be straight or bent.

From bottom: burnishers, bezel pusher, prong pusher

ADHESIVES

If you want to use an adhesive to join jewelry components, choose one that bonds quickly and stays strong. A colorless adhesive is generally preferable. Two-part epoxy comes in two vials or syringes, the contents of which combine to form a very strong bond. Epoxies work well on a wide variety of materials including metal, plastic, rubber, leather, stone, glass, and ceramics. Follow the manufacturer's directions to mix the specific proportions of the two parts together, stirring it with a wooden tongue depressor, and applying it quickly. Use epoxies in a

KEN THIBADO
Bulb Bracelet, 2003
7½ x 2¾ x 1³⁄₁₆ in. (19 x 7 x 3 cm)
Lightbulbs, fine silver, sterling silver
Photo by Robert Diamante

well-ventilated area and avoid breathing the fumes. Cyanoacrylate glues bond similar and dissimilar materials instantly—including your skin—so use them with care.

Soldering Tools & Materials

Soldering is another technique you can use to construct and connect jewelry components. It requires using a torch and solder to heat and bind metal.

Soldering station, from left: pickle pot, copper tongs, tripod, firebrick, third arm, flux, torch, striker, solder pick

FIREBRICK

Soldering must be done on top of a surface that is heat-resistant. One way to create this surface is with a layer of firebrick. These are the same bricks used inside ceramic kilns, and they can be purchased from any home improvement center.

SOLDERING TORCH

To solder you must have heat, and this heat is most often produced by a flame. This flame comes from a torch where a gas and either air or oxygen combine and are lit. The most easily accessible and reasonably priced gas to use for soldering is propane, although acetylene, which burns hotter than propane, is also very popular. Two separate tanks, one for the gas and one for the air or oxygen, are required. Each is fitted with a regulator used to set and maintain

DIANE A. ARCHER
Lake Erie Neckpiece, 1998
Pendant, 2 x 3½ x ¼ in. (5.1 x 8.9 x 0.6 cm)
Photoetched topographical map, sterling silver, beach rock; fabricated
Photo by artist

pressure and gas flow. Individual hoses, color-coded for safety, are attached to the regulators and run to the torch handle. A tip is attached to the handle to shape the size of the flame.

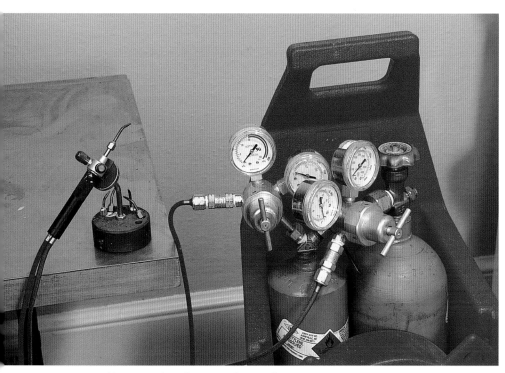

Soldering torch and oxy-acetylene tanks

SOLDERING FLUX

Solder flows only on a clean metal surface. If oxygen reaches the surface of the metal when it is heated, oxides form. Flux is a substance that promotes the fusion of metals by forming a layer that blocks the oxygen. Before soldering, use a paintbrush to apply flux to the surfaces to be joined to facilitate their union. Different types of flux are effective at different heat levels, most commonly between 1,100° and 1,500° F (600° and 800° C). Be sure to use the flux that corresponds to your soldering temperature.

SOLDER

Solder is a metal or a metallic alloy that, when melted, joins metallic surfaces. Different types of metal and different processes require the use of different solders. Gold and silver solders, alloyed to a lower melting temperature than the metals they join, are the most common. Within these two main categories there are several varieties of solder based on the temperature at which they melt, also know as their flow point. For silver solders, the most common are extra easy, easy, medium, hard, and IT (listed in order of increasing flow point). Gold solders are identified by their karat (generally 10, 14, or 16). Lower karat gold solders have lower melting temperatures than higher karat gold solders. Although the flow points for

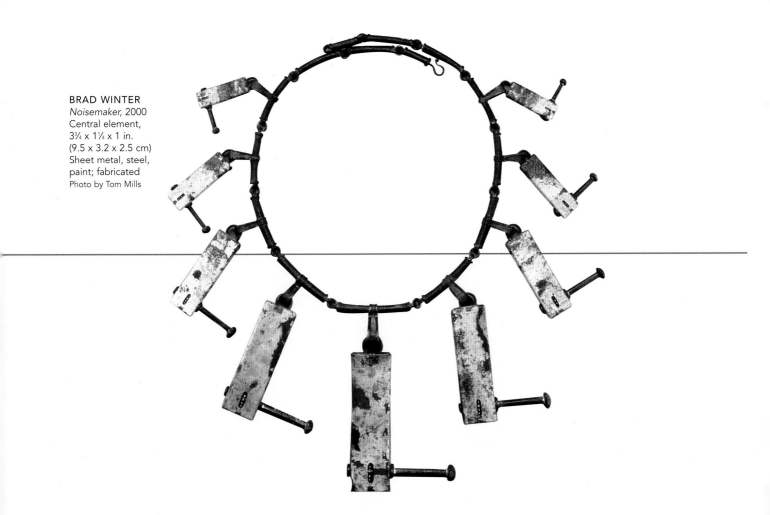

BRAD WINTER
Noisemaker, 2000
Central element,
3¾ x 1¼ x 1 in.
(9.5 x 3.2 x 2.5 cm)
Sheet metal, steel,
paint; fabricated
Photo by Tom Mills

silver solders are standardized (see chart on page 157), the flow points of gold solders may vary from manufacturer to manufacturer, so when placing your order, request a data sheet from your supplier. Solder is sold in several forms, the most popular being wire and sheet. Choose the type you like best for the soldering method needed.

PICKLE

Pickle is an acidic compound that removes flux and oxidized surfaces from soldered metal. Many varieties can be used, the most common being sodium bisulphate, which is also used to clean swimming pools. This chemical is available from jeweler's supply stores. Nontoxic substitutes include alum or a solution of vinegar and salt. To obtain the fastest results, use pickle that's been heated in a slow cooker dedicated to this process.

Finishing Tools & Materials

The surface of metal can take on many different appearances. It can be smooth and reflective, matte and lightly textured, and darkened with a patina. Taking steps to alter the appearance of a metal surface is a process known as finishing.

SANDING PAPERS & SCRUBBERS

Abrasive papers used to sand metal are made differently from those for sanding wood. Their grit is attached to the paper with a stronger fixative. This bond allows the abrasive to effectively shape and finish the metal, increases the paper's working life, and gives it the ability to be used both wet and dry. Metal sanding papers come in many grit sizes from coarse to fine. Higher numbered papers have finer grits. Most jewelers prefer 220-, 400-, and 600-grit papers. Use them in accordance with specific finishing tasks,

gradually working with finer and finer grits if a smooth finish is desired. Green kitchen scrub pads and different grades of steel wool are also commonly used for sanding and finishing metal.

PATINAS

Applying a patina is a simple process that adds depth and color to metal, especially if its surface is textured or has a design. Three solutions you can use to create a colored finish on metal are liver of sulfur, selenium toner, and black patina. You can purchase liver of sulfur and black patinas from jewelry suppliers, while selenium toner is sold at photography stores. Always read and follow the manufacturer's instructions when working with chemical patinas.

JEWELRY FINDINGS

Certain components simply ease the jewelry-making process, while others are needed to make finished pieces wearable. These elements are called findings. Jewelry and beading supply stores and catalogs sell an incredible variety of mass-produced findings for those who do not wish to make their own. Commercial findings come in lots of different metal types, including gold, gold-filled, sterling silver, brass, and surgical steel. Findings that can ease construction include settings, bezels, bead and end caps, crimp beads, jump rings, head pins, and eye pins. Findings that make a piece wearable include bails, clasps, pin backs, ear wires, ear posts, and nuts. More information on specific components can be found on pages 47–50.

Sanding pads, steel wool, sandpapers, sanding sticks

jewelry skills & techniques

When creating jewelry from found objects, you'll draw on a set of basic metalworking skills, such as sawing, piercing, riveting, and soldering. If you are new to jewelry making, the techniques that follow will give you a good foundation. Read through the different procedures carefully, then give them a trial run. They will become easier with practice. When making the projects later in the book, refer to this section to refresh your knowledge as needed.

Sawing Metal

To saw metal, you'll need a jeweler's saw and saw blades, a bench pin, and sheet metal. If you're new to this process, I recommend practicing on scrap sheet.

Installing a Saw Blade into a Saw Frame

1. Open the saw frame's jaw approximately 10 mm shorter than the length of the blade. Insert the blade into the top nut of the frame, with the teeth facing away from the neck and pointing down. Tighten the nut.

2. Rest the end of the saw frame handle on your sternum, and rest the top edge of the saw frame against the edge of a worktable or jeweler's bench. Use your sternum to press the saw handle and slightly shorten the length of the jaw.

3. Place the free end of the saw blade into the lower nut and tighten (see photo). Release the pressure on the saw handle. The blade should be stretched tight in the frame.

SAWING STEPS

1. Hold the saw in your hand lightly. Only use it as a guide and do not exert pressure. The temptation to press too hard is great, and most beginning metalworkers break a lot of saw blades. Don't worry if this happens to you. Success and ease comes through practice.

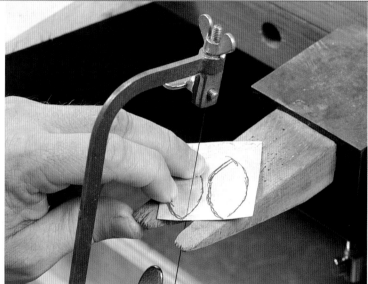

3. Turn the metal, not the saw frame, when making a rounded cut. To make a tight rounded cut, simultaneously turn the metal and the saw while quickly moving the frame up and down as shown.

2. Place the metal on the bench pin. Position the saw blade at a 90-degree angle to the metal. Move the saw frame up and down, keeping the frame pointing forward (see photo). The teeth of the blade will cut the metal only on the downward stroke.

Piercing Metal

Piercing metal is a three-step process. It consists of drilling a hole, feeding a saw blade through the hole, then sawing a shape in the surface of the sheet.

MATERIALS
Sheet metal

TOOLS & SUPPLIES
Steel block
Center punch
Chasing hammer
Small drill bit
Flexible shaft machine
Scrap block of wood
Jeweler's saw and saw blades

STEP BY STEP

1. Place the sheet metal on the steel block. Position the center punch at the point where you want to drill the hole. Use the hammer to lightly strike the top of the center punch or press down to release the hammer if using an automatic punch. This will create a dimple, or small indentation on the metal, that guides the drill bit and prevents it from sliding over the metal and marring its surface.

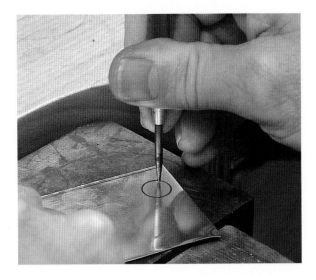

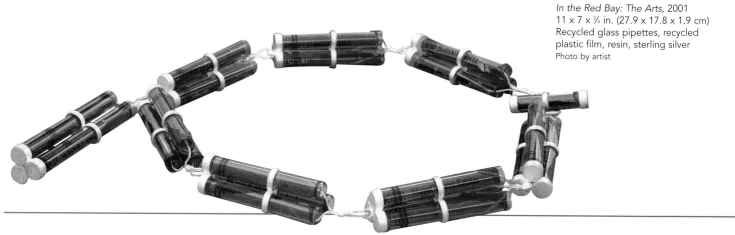

EMIKO OYE
In the Red Bay: The Arts, 2001
11 x 7 x ¾ in. (27.9 x 17.8 x 1.9 cm)
Recycled glass pipettes, recycled plastic film, resin, sterling silver
Photo by artist

2. Insert a drill bit into the flex shaft. Place the dimpled sheet metal on the wood block and drill the hole.

4. Reattach the blade to the frame. Saw the metal to cut out the interior shape.

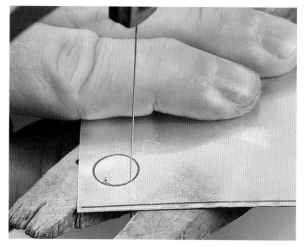

3. Detach the bottom end of the saw blade from the frame. Thread this end through the drilled hole.

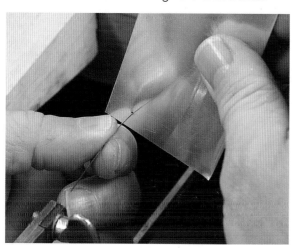

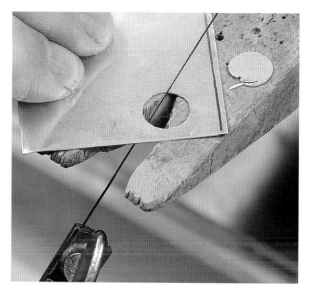

Filing Metal

All sawed metal pieces have sharp edges that
should be removed with a file for safe handling.
Metal can also be shaped and contoured with a file.

1. Secure the metal to be filed against a worktable
or bench. Select the coarsest file needed to begin
taking away the metal.

2. Place your index finger on the top of the file.
Press down as you slide the file forward against the
metal. Lift the file off the metal as you bring it back
and reposition it for another stroke (see photo).

Note: The teeth on the file are angled away from
the handle. This means that all cutting is accom-
plished on the file's forward stroke. Any pressure
applied on the back stroke only wears down the file.

3. Repeat steps 1 and 2 with a sequence of finer
files to complete the process.

Forming & Annealing Metal

To form sheet metal is to coax it into a dimensional
shape. There are many techniques you can use to
accomplish this. Bending by hand is perhaps the
most simple. Other options include hammering
sheet around a mandrel (see page 30, photo A) or
into a depression, using a dapping block and dap
(see page 30, photo B), forging, and using a die
press. When metal is formed, especially with a hammer, its molecular structure changes. The longer it's
worked, the harder and more brittle it becomes.
This change is called work hardening and it can be
reversed through the process of annealing.

Annealing loosens the molecular structure of
hardened metal to make it malleable once again.
Different metals are annealed in different ways,
but they are all based on heat. To anneal silver
and gold alloys, paint a paste flux onto the metal,
place it on a fire-resistant surface, and heat it to

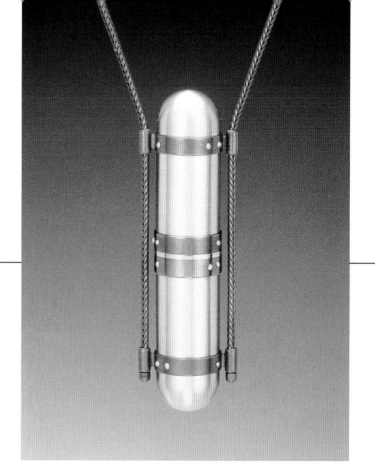

ABRASHA
Carbon Dioxide Necklace #2, 1994
2⅝ in. (6.7 cm) in diameter
Steel carbon dioxide cartridge, sterling silver,
18-karat gold, 24-karat gold; fabricated,
cold connected, riveted
Photo by Ronnie Tsai

approximately 1,100° F (600° C). At the correct annealing temperature, the flux liquefies and turns clear—a good visual indicator. Allow the piece to slightly cool until any reddish hue disappears, then use tongs to quench the annealed metal in water. When annealing copper, heat the metal until it glows dull red before quenching. Brass should be heated until it is clearly red-hot, allowed to cool for a minute, then quenched.

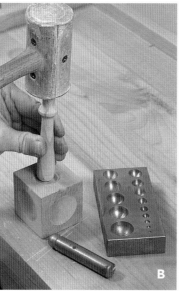

Making Cold Connections

Jewelry elements can be joined in many ways without soldering. These methods are called cold connection techniques and include riveting, using jump rings, wire wrapping, sewing, and adhesives.

Riveting

A rivet is a piece of wire or tube fed through a hole and flared on each end to hold two pieces of metal together. Rivets are very practical, attractive ways to cold connect found object jewelry.

MAKING A WIRE OR TUBE RIVET
MATERIALS
Sheet metal to be joined
Wire or tubing for rivet

TOOLS & SUPPLIES
Calipers (preferred) or metal ruler
Jeweler's saw and saw blades
Wet/dry sandpaper
Drill bit, same diameter as wire or tube rivet
Steel block
Center punch
Chasing hammer
Flexible shaft machine or small motorized rotary tool
Flaring tool, for tube rivets only

HARRIETE ESTEL BERMAN
Identity Beads, 2001
Largest bead, 2⅝ in. (6.7 cm) in diameter
Recycled UPC tin from post-consumer steel
cans, thermoplastic, brass, sterling silver,
10-karat gold, electrical wire, polymer clay
Photo by Philip Cohen

STEP BY STEP

1. Use calipers or a ruler to measure the combined thickness of the metals to be joined. Add approximately 2 mm to this measurement.

2. Use the jeweler's saw to cut a corresponding length of wire or tube. Sand the ends of the cut wire or tube.

3. Using a bit that is the same diameter as the wire or tube (see photo C), drill a hole through each metal piece at the point they are to be riveted as shown in photo D. (Refer to pages 27 and 28 for basic drilling instructions.) Thread the wire or tube through the drilled holes and place the metal on top of a steel block.

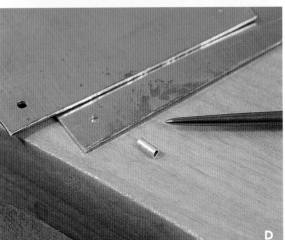

LAURA BEAMER
Vinyl Record Jewelry, 2004
Bracelet, 7½ x ⅝ x ⅛ in. (19 x 1.6 x 0.3 cm)
45-rpm records, sterling silver;
punched, riveted
Photo by artist

4. For wire riveting: Gently tap one end of the wire two or three times with a chasing hammer (see photo A). Turn over the metal piece and adjust the wire so there is an equal length sticking out of each side of the hole. Gently tap two or three times on the reverse side. Repeat this process—tapping, turning, and adjusting—until the wire ends flare (see photo B), forming the rivet and making a secure connection.

tap gently and directly on the tubing with the ball side of the chasing hammer as shown in photo E. Repeatedly turn the metal over in order to tap an equal amount on both sides until the rivet is secure.

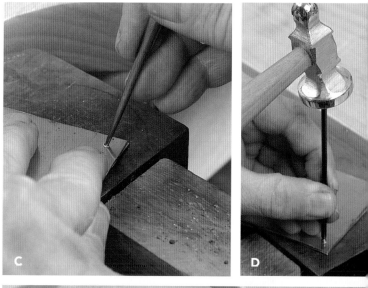

For tube riveting: Insert a flaring tool into one end of the tubing as shown in photo C. Use a chasing hammer to make one light tap on the flaring tool (see photo D). Turn over the metal piece, insert the flaring tool into the opposite tubing end, and make another light tap. Repeat this process, adjusting the tube so an equal length sticks out of each side of the hole, and make one tap on each tubing end until the tubing cannot be removed from the hole. At this point,

ANGELA GLEASON
Bread and Roses (Rosary), 2000
4 x ¾ x 7 in. (10.2 x 1.9 x 17.8 cm)
Political buttons, silver; fabricated
Photo by Hap Sakwa

Jump Rings

Wire circles, known as jump rings, are a simple way to hold jewelry components together. The rings are split so they can be opened and closed with pliers. Although jump rings are commercially available, you can easily make them yourself from almost any gauge wire.

MAKING JUMP RINGS

MATERIALS

Wire, gauge of your choice

TOOLS & SUPPLIES

Mandrel, diameter equal to the size jump rings you
   wish to make
Wire snips
Jeweler's saw and saw blades
Pliers

JAN ARTHUR HARRELL
Gold and Rust, 2003
2¾ x 2 x ½ in. (7 x 5.1 x 1.3 cm)
Sterling silver, copper, enamel, rust,
24-karat gold, crystal
Photo by Jack Zilker

STEP BY STEP

1. Cut a piece of wire and coil it tightly around the mandrel as shown. (Each full wrap makes one jump ring.) Slide the wire coil off the mandrel. If the coil is longer than 1 or 1½ inches (2.5 or 3.8 cm), trim it down so it will be easier to hold and saw.

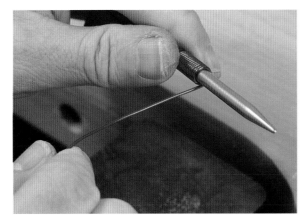

2. Hold the coil in your fingers on top of the bench pin. Use your other hand to hold the jeweler's saw at a slight angle. Carefully saw down the length of the coil.

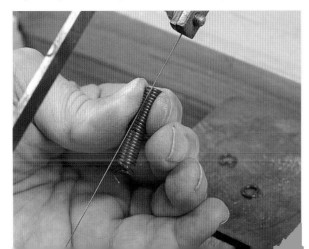

USING JUMP RINGS

• To open and close a jump ring, move its ends from side to side on the same plane.

• Only open a jump ring as far as needed to insert the objects being joined, otherwise the ring's shape can become distorted.

Wire Wrapping

Wire is versatile, readily accessible, and simple to use in cold connected jewelry. You can bend, wrap, sew, crochet, knit, twist, loop, and coil wire around found objects. Given the broad range of wire colors and gauges available, a well-designed wrap can be a highly decorative as well as functional jewelry element. Wire wrapping requires very few tools. All you need is an assortment of pliers and wire cutters or a jeweler's saw. You can adapt many popular techniques used for wrapping beads to work with found objects.

Wire wrapping two found objects

JO-ANN AIKEN
Mr. French, 2002
10 x 13 x 17 in. (25.4 x 33 x 43.2 cm)
Gold wire, gold leaf, opal, pearl, railroad nail, found copper, old jewelry items, devil's claw, glass marbles, human hair, dog fur, welding splatters, chandelier base, epoxy
Photo by David Egan

JO-ANN AIKEN
Mr. French (brooch detail)
3½ x ⅝ x ½ in. (8.9 x 1.6 x 1.3 cm)
Gold wire, pearl, railroad nail, epoxy
Photo by Norman Watkins

MATERIALS

Metal components to be joined
Soldering flux
Solder (hard, medium, and easy)

TOOLS & SUPPLIES

Safety glasses
Scrub pad or abrasive paper
Heat-resistant surface
"Third-arm" tweezers
Small paintbrush for applying soldering flux
Propane or acetylene soldering torch
Sharp tweezers
Copper tongs
Warmed pickle in pot, such as a slow cooker

Soldering

Hot metalworking often involves soldering. This process permanently joins two pieces of metal together with heat, flux, and solder. Practicing this technique is the best way to learn and perfect the process. Follow these steps to ensure a strong and good-looking solder joint. (The how-to photographs illustrate pick soldering.)

Soldering Kit

There are specific tools and materials you'll use every time you solder. To abbreviate the length of the supply lists in the projects chapter, refer to the kit to the right when you prepare to solder.

STEP BY STEP

1. Use a scrub pad or abrasive paper to clean the two metal elements to be soldered. Place them on top of a heat-resistant surface. Position the metal so the seam to be joined is flush. Use a paintbrush to apply flux to the seam (see photo).

the basics **35**

MASAKO ONODERA
Flowers for Daydreaming, 2004
2 x 1 x 1 in. (5.1 x 2.5 x 2.5 cm)
Sterling silver, earplugs
Photo by TTU Photo Services

2. Use the flux-coated brush to pick up the small solder pieces, called pallions, and apply them across the fluxed metal seam. Alternately, heat the pallions on top of the firebrick with the torch until they ball up and place them on the seam with a pick as shown.

3. Wearing safety glasses, light the torch, adjust the air to make a soft flame, and gently heat the area around the joint. The flux will bubble as the temperature rises (see photo). Use tweezers or a pick to reposition any solder that moves off the seam or to add additional solder.

ROBERT W. EBENDORF
Ring, 2002
¾ x ¾ in. (1.9 x 1.9 cm)
18-karat gold, diamond, old
English china shard
Photo by Bobby Hansson

ANIKA SMULOVITZ
Herbarium Specimen Ring, 2003
1⅜ x ¾ x ¾ in. (3.5 x 1.9 x 1.9 cm)
Sterling silver, glass, specimen
Photo by artist

4. Continue heating the piece until the solder flows bright and shiny around the joint as shown. Turn off the torch. Use copper tongs to quench the soldered metal in a pickle bath. Remove the metal from the acid, rinse it in cold water, and dry it.

Different soldering operations may require the use of different soldering techniques. You may find it easier to use a length of wire solder when connecting a large joint that requires a lot of solder. The wire is placed on the joint once the metal is properly heated, making it less likely than pallions or balls to move out of position. Sweat soldering will be beneficial when you need to permanently attach a smaller metal piece on top of a larger one or to attach findings.

SOLDERING TIPS

- Solder will only work if the metal joint is fully flush and properly aligned. It will never fill in a gap in a seam.
- Solder will only flow on clean metal.
- The metal must be heated sufficiently for solder to flow.
- Heat flows toward cooler metal. Counter this by directing the torch flame around the seam first, not directly at the joint.
- Solder always flows toward the heat. If metal is unevenly heated, the solder will not stay in the correct position.
- Both solder and flux are only effective within a very specific temperature range. Do not overheat the metal.
- Solder in dim light if possible, so you can see and react to the color changes of heated metal.
- Use "third arm" tweezers to balance awkwardly shaped metal pieces so they sit properly and remain stable during soldering.
- When soldering multiple seams, join the first seam with a hard solder (high melting point) and decrease the solder flow point as more seams are added. By doing this, the first seams remain intact when the piece is reheated.
- Store solders by type (soft, medium, and hard) and away from dirt and grease.

Special Skills for Found Objects

If you have an imaginative idea for using found materials, you don't have to settle for simply gluing them to surfaces or on findings. If you envision a strand of river stones on a necklace or sea glass sparkling from ear wires, there are ways to fabricate your ideas.

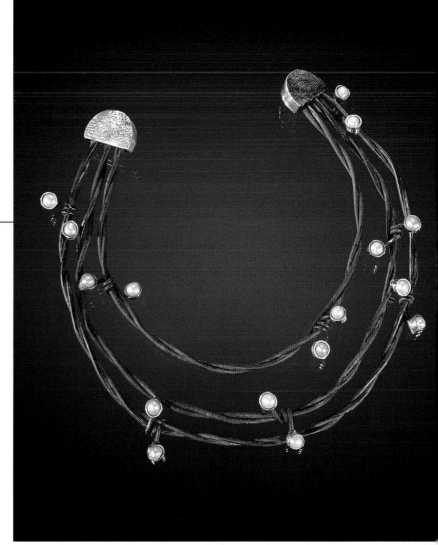

Found Metals

One of the pleasures of creating jewelry from found objects is the hunt for out-of-the-ordinary materials. You may find useable materials on the street—a flattened bottle cap, a rusty washer, or a shiny piece of metal. What do you do with such diverse metals? Well, you use them, but there are a few cautionary things to mention about working with such metals.

Identifying Metal

An easy way to determine if found metal is ferrous or nonferrous is to use a magnet. A magnet will not stick to nonferrous metals such as silver, gold, bronze, copper, tin, aluminum, pewter, or brass. If a magnet sticks to a metal that looks like copper or brass, it's plated metal.

Some bits and pieces of costume jewelry may be made of precious metal. As mentioned in the preceding paragraph, however, a silver or gold color doesn't guarantee that the item is a precious metal. Sterling silver and gold are hallmarked; if not, the item is probably plated with precious metal. If the metal is hallmarked, you can solder it after removing all embellishments such as stones. If the metal isn't hallmarked, your most reliable working methods will be cold connections.

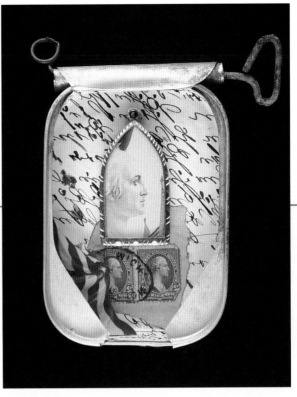

Preserving Surfaces

The patinas of aged metal are alluring. Silver takes on a dulled, gray tone that can be more appealing than a highly polished surface. Copper and bronze items exposed to the forces of nature develop a soft verdigris color. And then there's the expressive patina of rust on ferrous metals or the combination of rust and painted surface on a piece of old, lithographed tin.

To best preserve a patinated surface, avoid using heat processes and excessive handling. Use cold connections with surfaces that are patinated. A very light coat of microcrystalline wax can preserve patinas on silver, bronze, or copper. It's also possible to slow down flaking rust with a light application of acrylic sealer. Both the wax and the acrylic sealer will somewhat alter the original appearance of the patina.

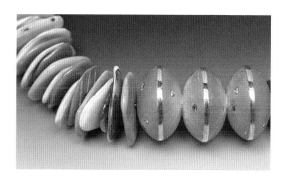

Drilling

Making a hole in a solid object is easy to accomplish, you simply need to consider the material through which you want to drill. For many applications, such as wood, plastic, shells, or bone, all you need is an appropriate size bit with an electric or hand drill. For more difficult materials, like rock, glass, and ceramic, you'll need diamond-coated drill bits and a few other items. Remember the number one rule for successful drilling: allow the drill bit to do the work. Light, steady pressure is all you need. Excessive force will cause one or two unwelcome events: the found object will break or the bit will break inside the object.

Drilling Glass, Ceramic & Stone

Drilling through hard materials requires diamond-coated bits. They're not terribly expensive. They may, however, wear out faster than regular hardened steel drill bits, so always have more than one on hand.

You can drill holes in ceramic shards and stones up to ⅜ inch (9.5 mm) thick with a handheld motorized drill and diamond drill bits. If you have access to a variable speed drill, use it. To drill holes in thicker stones, it's best to use a drill press with a motorized drill. That way, the hole through the stone is more likely to be drilled straight and true. Drilling through hard materials creates heat. The heat a drill bit generates can crack materials such as glass and stone. To avoid creating heat, you'll need to cool the materials as you work. The simplest way to cool a drill bit and found object is with water.

DRILLING A HOLE IN STONE

MATERIALS
Stone, up to ⅜ inch (9.5 mm) thick

TOOLS & SUPPLIES
Safety glasses
Small, shallow plastic container
Small block of wood
Sticky wax, florist's clay, modeling clay (optional)
Diamond-coated drill bit, ¹⁄₁₆ inch (1.6 mm)
Beeswax or burr lubricant
Flexible shaft machine or electric drill

STEP BY STEP
1. Put on safety glasses! Period. Don't attempt to drill through breakable materials without them.

2. Fill a small, shallow plastic container with water. Set it to the side.

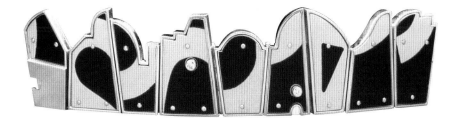

ROY
Mediterranean Bracelet, 1993
1½ x 6⅝ x ³⁄₁₆ in. (3.8 x 16.8 x 0.5 cm)
Street signs, diamonds, silver;
fabricated, hinged
Photo by Dean Powell

3. Place the stone on the block of wood to protect your work surface. You can hold the stone on the block with your fingers, or if you're uncomfortable holding the stone, use sticky wax or clay to secure it to the block.

4. Touch the drill bit to the beeswax or lubricant to lightly coat it. Start drilling with the flex shaft at a slight angle. Lightly touch the bit to the stone to nick its surface as shown. This prevents the bit from sliding away from where you want to drill the hole.

5. Slowly bring the flex shaft upright and lightly apply pressure to the nicked surface to start the hole (see photo A). Don't attempt to drill through the stone in one pass. As you drill, lift the bit to allow the debris to rise to the surface (photo B). Rinse the stone in the water, then dip the drill bit into the water to cool it. Every so often, touch the bit to the beeswax or lubricant before continuing to drill.

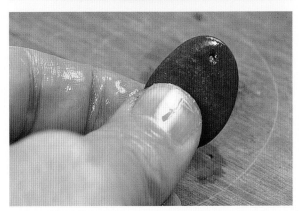

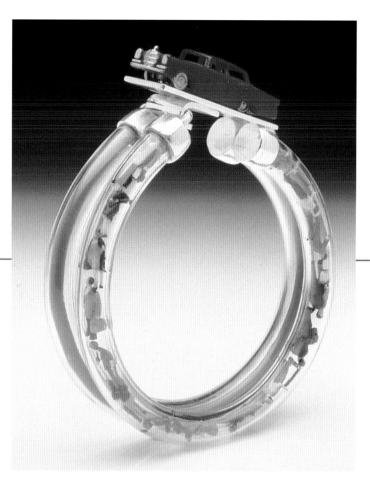

6. If needed, use a series of gradually larger diamond-coated drill bits or core bits to enlarge the hole.

Tip: When using a drill press, set the block of wood into the plastic container filled with water. Then place the container on the table of the drill press. The wood block will prevent you from drilling through the water-filled container.

Plastics

Using plastics, such as acrylic, laminates, and resins, is an innovative and easy way to inject a dose of color and transparency into found object jewelry.

NICOLE JACQUARD
Barbara, 2001
5½ x 5½ x ¼ in. (14 x 14 x .6 cm)
Silver, thermoplastic, 22-karat gold,
tulip petals, garnet
Photo by Kevin Montague

Acrylic Sheet

Acrylic is available in clear, transparent, and opaque sheets and in precut shapes. When working with acrylic sheet or shapes, always leave the paper masking film on the plastic as long as possible. Except for intricate detail work, you should remove the masking only when your project is completed.

If you purchase acrylic sheet from your local glass shop or home improvement store, have them cut it to size or close to the size you need. Then use a jeweler's saw to cut the acrylic to the exact size or shape you need (see photo A).

CUTTING ACRYLIC SHEET

If you need to cut down a full sheet, here's a simple method similar to that used to cut glass. Use it to cut acrylic sheet up to ³⁄₁₆ inch (5 mm) thick.

MATERIALS
Acrylic sheet

TOOLS & SUPPLIES
Straightedge
Scribe, awl, or utility knife
Clamp (optional)

STEP BY STEP
1. Place a straightedge on the acrylic sheet and hold it firmly in place.

2. Score the sheet by drawing a scribe, an awl, or a utility knife along the edge of the straightedge several times (seven or eight times for a ³⁄₁₆-inch [5 mm] sheet).

ROBLY A. GLOVER
Lurc/Allurc; Pointed Bobber, 2003
24 x 24 x ½ in. (61 x 61 x 1.3 cm)
Sterling silver, plastic
Photo by artist

3. Clamp the sheet or firmly hold it under a straight-edge with the scored mark hanging just over the edge of a table.

4. Apply a sharp downward pressure to break the sheet along the scored line.

Drilling a Hole in Acrylic or Plastic

If you can find them, use plastic-cutting bits for drilling these materials. If not, follow these suggestions for using conventional drill bits.

- Use a slow to medium speed to drill plastics. High speeds cause the material to melt.
- As you drill, lift the bit to allow the debris to come to the surface (see photo A).
- Dip the drill bit into a small container of water as you work. Doing so prevents the bit from becoming too hot and melting the plastic.

FILING, SANDING & FINISHING ACRYLIC

Once you've sawn out an acrylic shape, use a smooth cut file to file its edges and remove tool marks. File only in one direction, then proceed to 120-grit sandpaper if needed. Use 220- and 400-grit wet/dry papers to finish the job. (Wrapping the sandpaper around a sanding block will help you keep the edges of the acrylic perpendicular, and your fingers won't get as tired.) Final polishing gives acrylic a high luster (see photo B). Power-driven buffing tools are recommended. A handheld motorized tool with a buffing wheel attachment also works well for this type of job. To rub out a scratch, be sure to sand an area larger than the scratch. Use fine-grit wet/dry sandpapers in a circular motion with a light touch and plenty of water.

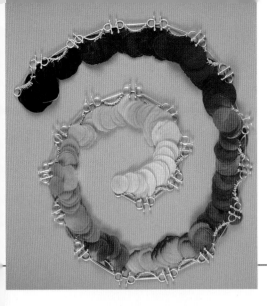

KRISTIN MITSU SHIGA
Since I Was Eight, 2001
66 in. (167.6 cm) long; largest
petal, 2 x 2½ in. (5.1 x 6.4 cm)
Sterling silver, pressed rose petals;
fabricated, laminated, riveted
Photo by Courtney Frisse

ALI FRIEDMAN
Seaglass Cuff, 2002
4 in. (10.2 cm) in diameter
Sea glass, sterling silver,
fine silver; fabricated
Photo by Steven Alfano

Laminating Film

Lamination sandwiches paper between two layers of plastic film. The laminate film protects paper from moisture, oil, wear, grease, and dirt. Lamination film is available in both gloss and matte finishes and is applied using either a hot or cold process.

Heat-sealed laminating film is usually found in commercial and school applications. Office supply stores carry heat-laminating systems or dry-mounting presses for small business use. Most copy shops provide inexpensive laminating services. Heat-sealed laminating films are usually thicker and more durable than cold-laminating films.

Cold-laminating film—clear adhesive shelf paper is one common type—requires no heat to seal the paper between the layers. There are several brands of clear adhesive papers available. Craft stores usually carry one or more brands of clear adhesive papers and cold lamination systems as well. The cold lamination systems sold in craft stores are easy to use at home. Several of these machines offer additional features, such as applying adhesives to paper items.

Tumbling

Do you want to give pieces of broken glass or pottery shards a soft, frosted surface? No problem.

You can achieve the look—to your exacting specifications—almost overnight. All you need are a pair of tile nippers, some eye protection, and a rock tumbler.

You can purchase rock tumblers in a variety of sizes at most toy or hobby shops. Tumblers have a rotary action and use an abrasive grit to simulate the action of ocean waves on glass, pottery, and rocks. (Though you can tumble rocks to a shiny, smooth finish—in fact, that's what most people use these machines for—a high polish won't occur overnight and may take up to a month to achieve.)

Rock tumbler, abrasive grit

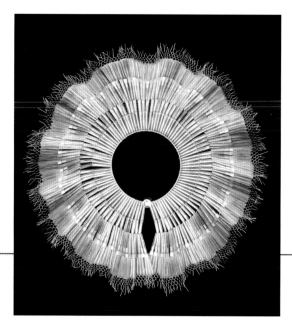

JAN YAGER
American Ruff, 2000
21 in. (53.3 cm) in diameter
Found plastic crack vials, coins,
sterling silver
Photo by Jack Ramsdale

Tumbling Glass or Ceramics

MATERIALS

Glass or ceramics

Coarse abrasive grit

TOOLS & SUPPLIES

Towel

Hammer

Safety glasses

Tile nippers

Rock tumbler

STEP BY STEP

1. Wrap the glass or ceramics inside a towel. Use a hammer to break the material into large shards. Don't mix the glass and ceramics. Tumble each separately for best results.

2. Wearing safety glasses, use the tile nippers to nip the shards into the general size and shape you need.

3. Following the manufacturer's instructions, fill or "charge" the tumbler. In general, you fill the barrel no more than three-quarters full of shards, then add the water and abrasive grit.

4. Tumble the shards overnight, then check the progress of the abrasive action. Some materials may require additional time to tumble.

5. When you are ready to empty the tumbling barrel, don't wash the grit down the drain. It will clog the pipes. Instead, rinse the grit from the shards and the barrel outside with a garden hose, or place the barrel in a bucket, rinse it indoors, and take the bucket outdoors to dispose of the dirty water.

Beading

A bead can be anything that has a hole through it. Wood, shell, glass, plastic, metal, clay, stone, paper, fabric—almost any material you can imagine.

There are many, many materials on which to hang or string beads. Bead thread is a strong, thin thread that resists fraying. Usually synthetic, it is perfect for both stringing and sewing beads. Monofilaments, tigertail (a tiny version of steel cable), and decorative threads such as leather, linen, satin, or silk can all be used to string beads. And don't forget found or repurposed materials such as rubber cord, string, ball chain, and even industrial wire.

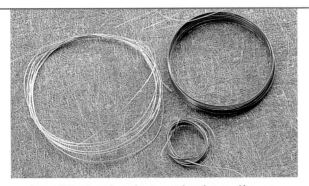

Traditional beading threads: tigertail and monofilament

From top: hemp, satin, rubber, leather, waxed linen

Colorful coated wire

If you're interested in doing more than simply hanging one bead on a cord or stringing a series of found objects, you'll find it helpful to gather a variety of findings to help you create jewelry. What follows is a brief listing of useful findings that you can purchase at your local bead shop or craft store.

Bead caps and **bead cones** hide the hole of the last bead in a strand and provide a finished look.

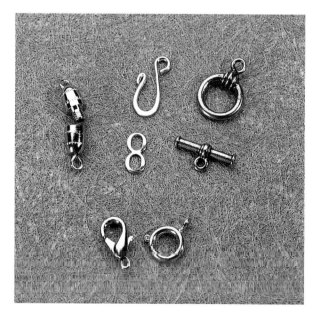

PAMELA MORRIS THOMFORD
My Father, My Children, My Worry:
A Mother's Prayer, 1999
40 x 2½ x ½ in. (101.6 x 6.4 x 1.3 cm)
Sterling silver, metal clay, ruby, mica,
photographs, rifle casings, coins,
copper, Red Cross medal; fabricated, cast, riveted, acid-etched
Photo by Tim Thayer

Eye pins (left) and **head pins** (right) are thin lengths
of wire on which you can string small beads. An eye
pin has a loop or eye at one end; a head pin has a
flat nail head on one end. Simply stack an assortment
of beads in a pleasing manner on an eye or head pin
(see photo A), then use needle-nose pliers to turn or
loop the loose end of the wire (see photo B).

Jump rings (see photo, page 33)
are wire circles that are useful
for connecting components
such as charms to a bracelet;
or they can be connected
together to form chains of
varying complexity.

Clasps for bracelets and necklaces are useful addi-
tions to your findings stash. They're available in a
variety of styles, including toggle, lobster claw, and
magnetic. Choose the ones you like best.

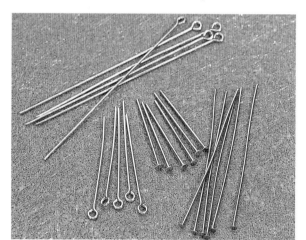

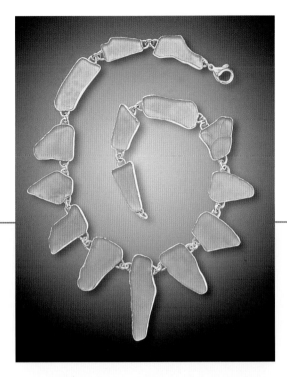

ALI FRIEDMAN
Seaglass Necklace, 2002
18 in. (45.7 cm) long
Sea glass, sterling silver,
fine silver; fabricated
Photo by Barry Blau

Clamshell beads (below, right) and **crimp beads** (below, left) are useful for single-strand jewelry. They hold and hide knots and supply loops for attaching clasp mechanisms. Clamshell beads are useful if your bead string is a knotable material; crimp beads are useful for tigertail and other materials that don't hold knots very well.

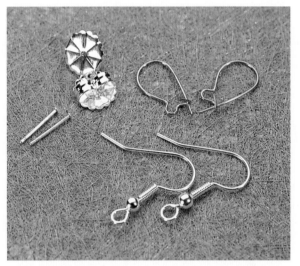

From left: ear posts, nuts, French wires, kidney wires

Have **French wires, kidney wires, clips, screws, nuts,** and **ear posts** on hand for finishing earrings. They're available at most bead stores in a variety of metals, such as stainless steel and sterling silver. You can also easily make your own French wires with a bit of sterling silver wire, a pair of round-nose pliers, and a small dowel or mandrel (see photo C).

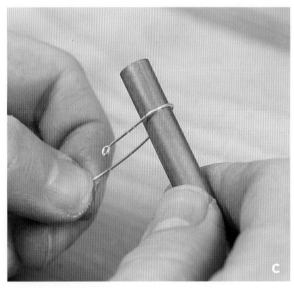

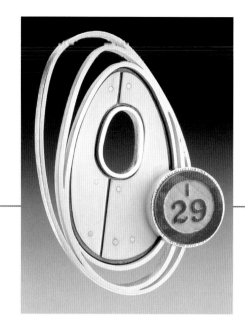

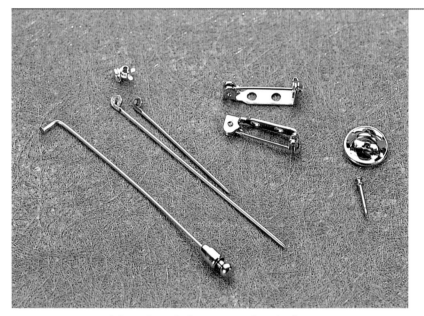

*From left: stick pin findings, assorted pin backs,
scatter pin clutch and post*

Base metal pin backs are available at most craft stores. They're easy to apply to the back of almost any creation with a dab of good jewelry glue or epoxy. A scatter pin clutch is a simple type of commercial jewelry finding used to secure brooch and pin posts. Truth be told, you can create a fabulous brooch with a single found object (say, a truly wonderful vintage aspirin tin), a pin back, and some glue (see photo, right). Viola! Instant jewelry.

the projects

Inspiring photographs, detailed step-by-step instructions, and insightful artist's comments are just a few of the special features accompanying these fabulous projects. Follow the directions as written to create a specific jewelry piece or use the ideas as starting points for your own found object design.

snappy cuffs & earrings

Create colorful cuffs out of can labels from exotic foods, cancelled stamps from envelopes, pages of old love letters, and even chopstick wrappers.

Materials
Recycled paper of your choice
Laminating film
Snap fasteners, for the cuffs
Ear wires, for the earrings

Tools & Supplies
Scissors or paper cutter
Tiny hole punch, for the earrings

Step by Step
FOR THE CUFFS

1 If needed, measure and cut rectangles out of the recycled paper you've selected. Using a paper cutter can help you cut evenly and squarely. An 8-inch length (20.3 cm) is an average size that fits most anyone. Men with larger wrists probably need a 9-inch length (23 cm). The width of the cuff is up to you. Those pictured range from 1⅛ inches (2.9 cm) wide (the cancelled-stamp cuff) to 3 inches (7.6 cm) wide (the condensed-milk label cuff).

2 You can laminate the recycled paper rectangle at home, but it's far easier to use the laminating machines at your local photocopy shop. These stores use a thicker grade of laminating film than the film available for home use. Once the paper is laminated, trim the film close to, but not against, the paper's edges.

3 Follow the manufacturer's instructions for setting the snap fasteners. When setting the snaps, pay close attention. You must place them correctly so they snap together.

FOR THE EARRINGS

1 Select a pair of cancelled stamps to use or cut two pieces of recycled paper. Have these materials laminated at your local photocopy shop.

2 Trim the laminated paper close to, but not against, the paper's edges. Use the hole punch to make a tiny hole near the top of each laminated earring. Thread the earrings onto ear wires.

Setting tool for snap fasteners

dumpster-drawer
necklace

Rummage through a stash of odds-and-ends and fasten together four found objects to create a one-of-a-kind necklace.

Materials

Two-part epoxy or other strong adhesive
Used plastic bicycle reflector
Found key-chain fob*
Metal vintage medal
Jump ring
Recycled chain

Tools & Supplies

Abrasive scouring pad (optional)
Wire snips
File
Pliers

* Most frequently associated with pocket watches, a fob
   also is any decorative or functional ornament attached to
   a key chain. Use a vintage or found key-chain fob as the
   base for the necklace. If you can't find one to recycle,
   purchase a new one from a key kiosk or home improvement center and distress it. To give the fob's surface a
   matte finish, scrub it with an abrasive scouring pad.

Step by Step

1 Follow the manufacturer's instructions to prepare
   the two-part epoxy or a similar strong-bonding
adhesive that conforms to irregular surfaces. Adhere
the plastic bicycle reflector to the key fob and let dry.

2 Use wire snips to remove any findings from the
   back of the vintage medal. File the surface flat
if needed.

3 Use the epoxy or strong adhesive to adhere the
   medal to the bicycle reflector. Let dry.

4 Use pliers to open the jump ring and attach the
   fob to the recycled chain.

CHECK IT OUT

Medals are awarded to both military personnel and civilians for
specific acts of bravery or merit. Often decorated with historical
or religious iconography, these medals lend themselves to rein-
terpretation for found object jewelry. Some vintage medals have
enameled surfaces, others are embossed in high relief, and a few combine
both color and depth. It can be interesting and insightful to research the
history of a found service medal before using it in a piece of jewelry.
The meaning of the medal may influence its use in your artwork.

beverage can
brooches

Turn the bottom of a recycled can into a brooch frame in which to display a collage of found objects.

Materials

Recycled beverage cans

Assorted found objects for collage, such as leather shoestrings (top), museum maps (right), river stones (left), or plastic compass (bottom)

Two-part epoxy

Other adhesives, like decoupage medium and polyester casting resin (optional)

Pin backs

Tools & Supplies

Snips or metal shears

Files

Sandpaper

Step by Step

1 Use the snips or metal shears to cut down one side of a recycled beverage can. (It's easiest to start the cut at the opening in the top of the can.) Stop cutting slightly above the beveled edge at the base of the can.

2 Continue to slowly and carefully trim the can off its base. Cut away any preprinted text or graphics from the can if you wish. Repeat steps 1 and 2 to make several "blank" brooch frames if desired.

3 Use files and sandpaper to smooth the edges of the can base and to level out any uneven areas. Wash the base to remove metal debris and any beverage residue.

4 Determine which found objects you want to collage inside the base and how best to adhere the objects to the metal. (The featured projects show several solutions. The paper map fragments and icons were affixed to the can base with decoupage medium. The leather shoelaces and the river stones were adhered with two-part epoxy. The plastic compass was embedded in clear polyester casting resin. Whatever adhesive you chose, remember to read and follow the manufacturer's instructions. Some adhesives, like decoupage medium, are nontoxic and simple to use; others, such as two-part epoxy and especially polyester resin, can be toxic and must be used with great care in a well-ventilated area.) Affix the found object collage to the can base and let dry.

5 Before attaching the pin back to the back of the can base, check the fit. You may have to slightly bend the pin back for it to conform to the curve of the can base. Use two-part epoxy to attach these elements and let dry.

CHECK IT OUT

Tin cans are actually steel cans coated with a microscopic layer of tin: one ton of cans consists only of 5 to 6 pounds (2.3 to 2.7 kg) of actual tin. The average person uses about 142 cans per year, and it takes 100 years for a single can to degrade. When you recycle one tin can, you save enough energy to keep a 100-watt light bulb lit for 3½ hours or to run your television set for 4 hours.

lost earrings
bib

Make partnerless earrings the focal point of a
necklace and you can enjoy them all over again.

Materials

Chain, such as the rolo or the belcher style, with broad and equal links (each approximately 4 mm), 8 to 10 inches (20.3 to 25.4 cm) long

Assorted jump rings, to match the chain

Assorted single earrings

Eye pins, heavyweight, 1½ inches (3.8 cm), to match chain

Head pins, heavyweight, 1½ inches (3.8 cm), to match chain

Assorted vintage beads

Assorted bead caps

Bead cones

Commercial clasp for a heavy necklace, such as a toggle or S-style

Tools & Supplies

Needle-nose pliers

Step by Step

1 Find the center of the chain. Use one or more jump rings to attach the showiest, longest stray earring or combination of earrings at this point. (For this project, the artist used a very large earring that was pierced on its bottom edge for dangles. She removed the original dangles and replaced them with several vintage pieces that made good focal points.)

2 Once the central element is in place, work up the sides of the chain. This process is basically trial and error, like putting a puzzle together. You might want to arrange a series of single earrings on your work surface and see how they look together. The length and style of the layout is completely up to you. Make layers by connecting several small items together if you wish. You can remove the back of a clip-on earring and wire it to another earring to make a custom dangle. Wire other found objects into the design if desired. Variation adds to the sense of the unexpected.

3 Continue attaching elements from both sides of the centerpiece until you are satisfied with the necklace and how it lays. Add as many earrings up the sides of the chain as you wish, leaving at least the last segment of the chain free of embellishment. This is where you will begin to attach the remainder of the necklace.

4 Decide how long you want the necklace to be. (The artist created a long, 24-inch [61 cm] necklace so the bottom of the centerpiece would fall in the middle of the chest.) To finish the necklace, use heavy 1½-inch (3.8 cm) eye pins to attach a series of commercial bead caps and cones along with some wonderful vintage beads. Finish the necklace by attaching the clasp of your choice.

"I can never walk away from an item that has flair, movement, and color. I have boxes full of items I've sorted into plastic storage bags—stray earrings, chain, broken jewelry, keys, photos, interesting mounts, connectors. I hate to see waste and I love old jewelry. Scout flea markets and yard sales for bags of single or broken earrings, glass beads, and other filler material. If you've inherited Mom's, Grandma's, and Aunt Ethel's old costume jewelry, cull through it and put the stuff that goes together in project bags for a rainy day. What wonderful memory jewelry you could make! Be bold and experiment with the unexpected!" BRENDA SUE LANSDOWNE

DESIGNER: **BRAXTON MORRIS**

junk mail
jewelry

Strip the trendy colors right out of the latest fashion catalogs or magazines to make these unique beads.

The Necklace
Materials

Old magazines or catalogs

Decoupage medium

Spacer beads of your choice, approximately ½ inch
(1.3 cm) in diameter or larger to protect the paper
beads, hole must fit over cord clasp (33 used in
pictured necklace)

Rubber necklace cord with clasp in length of your
choice (pictured necklace is 16 inches [40.6 cm])

Tools & Supplies

Paper cutter or craft knife and metal ruler

Small dowel, approximately ¼ inch (6 mm) in diameter

Fine-tip artist's paintbrush

Step by Step

1 Browse through old magazines or catalogs to
find printed images that appeal to you. Make
sure the colors and patterns you want to show on
the beads are at or near the edge of the page.

2 Use the paper cutter or a craft knife with a metal
ruler to cut uniform strips of paper, each ¼ x 6
inches (0.6 x 15.2 cm). It took 32 strips to make the
beads for this necklace, but cut more so you'll have
a variety of beads from which to choose.

3 Hold the end of one strip against the dowel.
Wrap the paper around the dowel once to meet
the strip end. Apply a small amount of decoupage
medium at this point and adhere the wrapped
paper, making sure all edges are straight. Briefly
hold the strip in this position until the glue slightly
bonds. Wipe off any excess glue.

4 Continue wrapping the strip around the dowel,
keeping the paper taut and straight, until you
reach the loose end. Apply decoupage medium to
the underside of the loose end and press it down,
adhering it to the wrapped paper. Wipe off any
excess glue. Set the bead aside to dry.

5 Repeat steps 3 and 4 to make more beads for
your necklace. Be sure to wrap the strips in such
a way that the side of the paper you want to show
remains exposed. After a few beads, you'll get the
hang of it.

6 String one spacer bead on the rubber cord,
then one paper bead. Repeat this sequence to
fill the full length of the cord as shown, ending with
a spacer bead. For a different look, string a smaller
number of beads on the cord.

K. DANA KAGRISE
Royal Flush, 2002
15 x 4 in. (38.1 x 10.2 cm)
Playing cards, aluminum rivets;
cold connected
Photo by Jeff Sabo, Miami University

junk mail
jewelry

The Earrings
Materials
2 eye pins
Old magazines or catalogs
Decoupage medium

Tools & Supplies
2 ear wires
Wire cutters
Paper cutter or craft knife and metal ruler
Fine-tip artist's paintbrush
Needle-nose pliers

Step by Step

1 Determine how long you want the paper bead dangles to be. The pictured earrings have paper beads that are 1⅛ inches (2.9 cm) long. Add approximately ¼ inch (6 mm) to this length. (You will later loop this excess wire.) Use the wire cutters to trim the straight ends of the eye pins to this length.

2 Select one or two printed images from a magazine or catalog that appeal to you. The colors and patterns in the images can be different for each earring if desired.

3 Use the paper cutter or a craft knife with a metal ruler to cut two long strips of the selected printed pages. To create graduated beads such as the ones pictured, cut a strip that is the full length of the bead on one end and very slowly and evenly tapers to a point at the opposite end. You may want to use two long strips per earring to build up a more angled bead. If so, partially taper the first strip and begin the second strip with a width equal to that of the first strip's narrower end. Then taper it to a point.

4 Tightly wrap the widest end of one paper strip around an eye pin once, making sure an edge is even with the loop at the bottom of the pin. Use the paintbrush to apply decoupage medium to the wrapped paper, and hold the paper together until a bond forms.

5 Continue to tightly wrap the strip around itself. Work slowly and evenly for the best results. Once you reach the end of the strip, secure it to the wrapped paper with decoupage medium.

6 If you are using only a single strip, set the bead aside and let the glue dry. If you are using two strips, adhere the widest end of the second strip in the center of the bead with decoupage medium, evenly wrap the remainder of the paper around the bead, secure the end with additional glue, and let dry.

7 Repeat steps 4 through 6 to create the second paper bead dangle.

8 Use the needle-nose pliers to create a loop in the excess wire at the top of each paper bead dangle. Slip the ear wires on the loops and secure.

triple-word-score
bracelet

Use word game tiles to create a provocative adornment that will get your "points" across.

triple word score
bracelet

Materials

Game tiles, approximately 8 per bracelet
Disposable plastic lid, small
Thick elastic beading cord
Embellishments, such as Milagros or
    vintage buttons (optional)
Rivets or tacks for attaching embellish-
    ments (optional)
Spacer beads of your choice
Clear nail polish

Tools & Supplies

Pencil
Scissors or craft knife
Flexible shaft machine
Small drill bits

Step by Step

1 Place one game tile on its side on top of the small plastic lid. Use the pencil to trace the side of the tile onto the lid. Cut out the traced shape with scissors to make a template.

2 Choose a drill bit that is slightly larger than the diameter of the elastic beading cord. Mark two points on the plastic template that are approximately ½ inch (1.3 cm) apart and equally spaced from the edges. Drill the marked points. You'll use this template to mark points on each of the game tiles.

3 Now comes the fun part: choose your word! A word of eight or nine letters works well. If you wish, use blank game tiles to indicate the beginning of a word or as a place on which to add embellishments.

4 Using the plastic template, mark both sides of each game tile. Drill through each tile at the marked points. Lay the tiles in a row. (Spelling counts!)

5 If you wish to add an embellishment to a blank game tile, do it now. As shown in the project photos, you can drill through the front side of the tile and use a rivet or rivets to connect an object (button, page 63), or you can simply secure it with a decorative tack (Milagros, above).

6 Cut two lengths of the elastic cord, each approximately 6 inches (15.2 cm) longer than the row of game tiles. Loosely knot together one end of the elastic cords.

7 Thread the first letter tile onto the two cords. Add one or more spacer beads, followed by the second letter tile. Repeat this step until you've spelled out your word.

8 Check the bracelet for fit. If needed, restring the letter tiles with additional bead spacers to increase the size of the bracelet.

9 Tie each pair of elastic cord ends together with a tight square knot. Coat each knot with clear nail polish, let dry, then cut off any excess cord.

Variations

String drilled mahjong tiles into bracelets or incorporate dice (remember, they come in cubes and polyhedrons). Also consider using dominos, old checkers, bingo tokens, small playing cards, Chinese chess markers, and poker chips. Or you might contemplate using small toy components such as building bricks, wooden blocks, doll parts, or puzzle pieces.

Some board games go hand in hand with their playing pieces. It's hard to imagine playing without them. However, some early board game manufacturers encouraged players to use household items such as buttons and pennies to move around the board.

Milagro means "miracle" in Spanish. In Latin America, milagros are also very small metal sculptures, typically silver, that spiritual believers attach to altars, statues, or effigies of saints as votive offerings. Milagros are believed to promote healing, romance, prosperity, and other requests. They are often in the shape of the afflicted body part or object of desire.

- Scour secondhand stores, flea markets, and yard sales for old, inexpensive games from which you can plunder the playing pieces.
- Look in gaming stores for unusual, modern playing pieces. Visit toy stores to sniff out charms or colorful little figures.
- Use different search terms such as "game pieces," "playing pieces," "game tokens," and "game markers" to find online auction sites that sell both vintage and new supplies, or search by the name of the game you wish to acquire.

bakelite button
pin & posts

Vintage or found buttons are easy to restyle into a fabulous retro jewelry set.

Materials

Vintage or found buttons, 1 for brooch, 2 for earrings

Acrylic sheet for background shapes (precut if desired)

Sterling silver sheet, 22 gauge

Sterling silver tubing, to fit holes in buttons*

Silver solder (hard and easy)

Sterling silver ear posts

Sterling silver pin stem

Tools & Supplies

Sandpaper, fine grade

Steel wool, very fine

Steel block

Center punch

Chasing hammer

Drill bits

Flexible shaft

Soldering kit, see page 35

Flaring tool

*Measure the diameter of the holes in the buttons before you purchase the silver tubing for this project. Or better yet, take the buttons with you when you purchase the tubing.

Step by Step

1 Design background shapes that compliment the vintage or found buttons, one shape for the brooch and one shape for each earring. Measure and mark the acrylic sheet with these shapes. Use the jeweler's saw to cut out the acrylic shapes, then lightly file the edges. Finish the edges with fine-grade sandpaper and very fine steel wool. (If you are using precut acrylic forms, this step is not necessary.)

2 Mark the 22-gauge sterling silver sheet with a backing shape for each of the cut acrylic forms. These silver shapes need only be large enough to hold the tube rivets and the soldered findings. Cut out the shapes with the jeweler's saw, and sand the edges.

3 Measure the combined thickness of each acrylic sheet and button set. Cut a length of the sterling silver tubing slightly longer than this measurement for each button's holes. File or sand smooth the ends of the cut tubing.

4 Choose a drill bit equal in diameter to the sterling silver tubing. (You may wish to use a drill gauge to accurately determine the size of the bit you need.) Mark and drill holes in each of the acrylic forms that match the placement of the holes in the buttons.

5 Mark the placement of the button holes on the silver backing sheets. Drill these holes slightly smaller than the tubing's diameter to ensure a tight fit.

6 Feed one small cut silver tube into each hole drilled on the silver backings. File the tubes as needed. Solder the tubing onto the silver backings with hard solder. Pickle and clean the metal.

7 Place each acrylic and button set on its soldered backing. Make any necessary adjustments. Remove the loose elements. Use easy solder to attach the earring posts and pin findings to their specific backing sheets. Pickle and clean the metal elements.

8 Slip the acrylic forms and buttons back onto the tubes. Flare the tube rivets and gently hammer them to secure. Fasten the pin stem to the brooch.

TRACK IT DOWN

- Use the replacement buttons that clothing manufacturers supply with their products.
- Dig through your own box of old buttons or those at a flea market or garage sale.
- Check the buttons on a worn-out coat, suit, or jacket before giving it away. You may want to turn them into fantastic jewelry.

made-to-measure accessories

Let the graphic qualities of measuring tapes inspire a whole line of new jewelry.

Materials

FOR THE CUFFS OR THE COLLAR

Fiber measuring tape, vintage or found
Sewing thread, invisible or colored
Clear nail polish
Snap fasteners
Assorted found buttons or other
  embellishments (optional)

FOR THE RING

Fiber measuring tape, vintage or found
Acrylic medium

Tools & Supplies

FOR THE CUFFS OR THE COLLAR

Scissors
Sewing machine with zigzag stitch

FOR THE RING

Scissors
Dowel, diameter equal to desired ring size
Plastic wrap
Paintbrush
Rubber bands

Step by Step

FOR THE CUFFS OR THE COLLAR

1 Measure and cut equal lengths of the
  measuring tape. The average length needed for a cuff is 8 inches (20.3 cm). Increase or decrease this length based on wrist size. Lay the lengths side by side on a flat surface as you cut them. If you wish to vary the position of the numbers on a multilayered cuff, you'll have to sacrifice some of the tape as you cut it. The measurement for the collar is based on neck size. A 15-inch (38.1 cm) collar fits an average neck.

2 Cut a couple of extra measuring tape
  lengths to use for practice before starting to sew. Thread the sewing machine. Adjust the stitch width to catch both pieces of the measuring tape. Adjust the stitch length as desired. Practice sewing until you are pleased with the results.

3 Stitch together lengths of the measuring
  tape to create the cuff or collar. Backstitch at the beginning and at the end of each row. Once the desired width is achieved, tie off the thread ends, trim them, and finish each end with a dab of clear nail polish.

4 The width of the cuff or collar will deter-
  mine how many snap fasteners are needed. Following the manufacturer's instructions, set one or more snap fasteners at each end of the cuff or collar.

5 Stitch found buttons or other
  embellishments on the cuff or collar as desired.

FOR THE RING

1 Cut a piece of measuring
  tape that is approximately 18 inches (45.7 cm) long. Wrap the dowel with a piece of plastic wrap.

2 Coil the measuring tape
  around the dowel one time. Brush acrylic medium onto the end of the tape to adhere it. Hold the tape with your fingers until the medium is dry.

3 Brush the ring with the acrylic medium,
  then continue to coil the measuring tape around the dowel. As you make each turn, brush the tape with a coat of the medium. Take care to align the edges as you wrap the tape around the dowel. Make the ring as thick as you desire.

4 Cut off the excess measuring tape. Secure
  the loose tape end in place with rubber bands. Allow the acrylic medium to dry overnight.

5 Remove the rubber bands and apply one or
  more coats of acrylic medium to the ring, paying particular attention to its edges. Allow the medium to dry.

chandelier crystal **lariat**

The lariat necklace design provides two open ends that are ideal for showcasing large found objects such as these chandelier prisms. Tie the ends tight for a choker style or keep the knot loose for a longer necklace.

Materials

Soft gold-filled wire, 22 gauge, 8 feet (2.4 m)

Vintage crystal beads, 4 mm, approximately 64

Soft gold-filled wire, 20 gauge, two 3-inch
(7.6 cm) lengths

2 vintage faceted crystal beads, approximately 8 mm

2 vintage crystal chandelier prisms, each
approximately 1¼ inches (3.2 cm) long

Tools & Supplies

Flush wire cutters

Chain-nose pliers

Round-nose pliers

Step by Step

1 Use the flush wire cutters to cut the 22-gauge wire into 64 pieces, each approximately 2 inches (5 cm) long. (As your wire wrapping skills develop, you may be able to use shorter lengths.)

2 To make the beaded wire links for the chain, use the chain-nose pliers and make a right angle close to the center of each 2-inch (5 cm) wire piece.

3 Lightly grasp the wire at the right angle with the round-nose pliers. Use your other hand to begin to form a loop by wrapping the wire around the top of the pliers.

4 Use the chain-nose pliers to lightly grasp the loop on both sides. Use your other hand to wrap the wire around the neck of the loop two to three times. When wrapping, pull tightly. Cut off the excess wire with the flush wire cutters.

5 Slip a 4-mm crystal bead onto the wire and make another right angle. Leave a little room above the bead for the wire wrap. Repeat steps 3 and 4 to make a second loop. Adjust the loops to face the same direction.

6 To add another beaded link, begin with making a loop (steps 2 and 3). Before wrapping the wire around the neck, slip the loop through the first completed beaded link, then loop it. Continue making the wire link as directed in steps 4 and 5. Repeat this step until you have a beaded chain that measures approximately 27 inches (68.6 cm) in length.

7 To make the wire-wrapped crystal dangles, cut two pieces of the 20-gauge wire, each 3 inches (7.6 cm) long. Begin to make a loop in the wire as directed in steps 2 and 3. Slip the loop on one of the ends of the chain, and wrap one wire end around the neck of the wire (as in step 4). Thread one 8-mm crystal bead on the wire.

8 Use the round-nose pliers to make a curved right angle bend approximately ½ inch (1.3 cm) below the 8-mm crystal bead. Thread a chandelier prism onto the wire and hold it in place next to the right angle. Use your other hand to push up the wire end to make another right angle. At this point, the wire will be in a U shape with the chandelier prism in the middle. Adjust the angles so the crystal moves freely. Center the wire end with the neck of the wire and wrap the end two to three times (refer to step 4). To finish the lariat, create one more crystal chandelier dangle on the other end of the beaded chain.

TRACK IT DOWN

- Poke around dumpsters in upper-crust neighborhoods when old buildings and homes are being renovated. You can "inherit" a wealth of jewelry materials!

"I always remember, as a child, staring up at the wonderful rainbow reflections that my grandmother's chandelier shined on the ceiling during her dinner parties. This beautiful Chandelier Crystal Lariat is a wonderful way to remember those festive and joyous celebrations." RACHEL DOW

icon brooch

Thoughtfully combine dissimilar materials such as wood, nails, and a tintype photograph to form an expressive piece of jewelry.

Materials

Brass or copper sheet, 18 gauge
Patina solution, green or blue
Quick-drying epoxy
Pin back
Driftwood, wood, or branch
10 to 14 small brass nails
2 small screw eyes
Gold or silver wire, thin
Assorted beads, pearls, or other found
   embellishments
Gem tintype photograph or laser-copied image
Grommet (optional)
Printed text
White glue
Head pin, 2 inches (5 cm)
2 split rings
Acrylic paints (optional)
Clear paste wax

Tools & Supplies

Jeweler's saw and saw blades
Sandpaper
Steel block
Center punch
Hammer
Flexible shaft
Small drill bits
Large sewing needle (optional)
Scissors
Paintbrush
Needle-nose pliers

Step by Step

1 Use the jeweler's saw to cut the brass or copper sheet into a rectangle that is approximately 1½ x 1¼ inches (3.8 x 3.2 cm). Sand the cut edges smooth and sand the surface of the metal to a dull finish.

2 Near each corner of one of the shorter ends of the metal rectangle, dimple, then drill a hole. These two holes will be used to hang the metal. Drill a third hole at the opposite end of the rectangle, centered and near the edge.

3 Apply the patina solution to the metal surface and let dry. To produce a more intense color, add a second layer of the patina solution to the dried metal surface. The more layers of color added, the darker the patina will appear.

4 Mix the quick-drying epoxy following the manufacturer's instructions. Use the epoxy to adhere the pin back to the back of the driftwood. Let dry.

5 Thread the screw eyes into the bottom edge of the wood, spacing them to match the distance between the holes in the top of the metal rectangle. (Tip: Use a large sewing needle to make pilot holes in the wood before screwing in the eyes if needed.)

6 Examine the driftwood and decide what embellishments would look interesting. Lightly tap the brass nails into the driftwood along its top edge. You may want to wrap the wood with wire, as shown in the photo, or add vintage pearls, beads, or small found objects. If adding decorative wire, wrap it around the opened pin back to provide additional security.

7 Apply the quick-drying epoxy to the back of the tintype photo and attach it to the metal rectangle. (This glue does not dry immediately, so do not walk away and expect the photo to remain in the correct position. Sometimes it can slip or move, so watch over it.) After the epoxy is dry, drill a small hole through the tintype and the metal and attach a decorative grommet if desired. (If you are using a laser-copied image, attach it to the metal with white glue. Add a little water to the glue if it seems too thick.)

8 Cut some interesting printed text to fit on the metal under the tintype. Attach the text clipping to the metal using white glue and a paintbrush.

9 String a bead or two onto the 2-inch (5 cm) head pin. Thread the pin through the bottom hole in the pendant and wrap the wire around itself. (If the bead is large enough, hide the end of the wire inside the hole of the bead.) Snip off any excess wire.

10 Use pliers to feed one split ring through each of the holes at the top of the metal pendant. Once connected, use pliers to attach the split rings on the pendant to the screw eyes on the bottom of the driftwood (one ring per eye). This may take some maneuvering, so be patient.

11 Use any acrylic paint, such as an old-gold metallic color, to touch up the brooch or to add highlights. Touch up the patina with a paint-brush as needed. Be careful not to get the patina on the tintype as it could obscure the image.

12 Use a paper towel to apply a thin covering of clear paste wax over the surface of the brass. Do not rub the surface too hard. You can cover the tintype, but do so slowly and gently.

CHECK IT OUT

Tintype photos contain no tin; in fact, they were made on thin, coated iron plates. Begun in 1855 in Worcester, Massachusetts, the process came from the patent-leather industry. Photographers made their own plates by painting them with gelatin and dipping them in a silver nitrate mixture. The plates were used while still wet. The prints were one of a kind and generally 2¼ x 3½ inches (5.7 x 8.9 cm). Tintypes were a uniquely American phenomenon, spread by the working class who could not otherwise afford photography. Early photographs cost one to 10 dollars; tintypes cost 10 to 25 cents.

fishing flies
bracelet &
earrings

Originally designed to attract fish, these flies can also attract attention when recycled and worn as a bracelet and earring set.

fishing flies
bracelet & earrings

Materials

Old fishing flies, medium size, approximately 30
Hypo cement*
Gold-filled wire, 22 gauge, 7 feet (2.1 m)
Vintage glass beads, 4 to 5 mm, approximately 16
Gold-plated toggle clasp
Vintage glass beads, 2 to 3 mm, approximately 30
Gold-plated ear wires

Tools & Supplies

Wire cutters
File
Chain-nose pliers
Round-nose pliers
Flush wire cutters

*Hypo cement is an ideal adhesive for fine detail work. It has a tiny applicator that makes it easy to apply glue to bead tips and knots.

Step by Step
FOR THE BRACELET

1 Using the wire cutters, carefully cut off the hooks from the fishing flies. Make sure to cut just below the fiber-wrapped section of the fly. Dab the end of the fibers with the hypo cement and let dry. Use the file to file off any metal burrs.

2 To make a 6¾-inch (17.1 cm) bracelet chain, cut approximately 12 pieces of the 22-gauge gold-filled wire. Each piece should measure approximately 2 inches (5 cm) in length.

3 Use the chain-nose pliers to make a right angle close to the center of one 2-inch (5 cm) wire piece.

4 With the round-nose pliers, lightly grasp the wire at the right angle and use your other hand to wrap the wire around the top of the pliers to begin to form a loop.

5 Using the chain-nose pliers, grasp the loop on either side. With your other hand, wrap the wire around the neck of the loop about two to three times. When wrapping the wire end, pull tightly. Cut off the excess wire with the flush cutters.

6 Thread a 4- to 5-mm bead onto the wire, and make another right angle. Leave a little room above the bead for wrapping the wire. Repeat steps 4 and 5 to make the loop. When the second loop is finished, adjust the loops so they face the same direction.

7 To add another beaded link, begin with making a loop (steps 3 and 4). Before wire wrapping, slip the loop through the loop of the first completed link. Continue with steps 5 and 6 to complete the link. Repeat this step, adding links until the beaded chain measures approximately 6¾ inches (17.1 cm) in length.

8 Attach the toggle clasp to the ends of the bracelet chain. Adjust the loops before wrapping the ends so the clasp moves freely. The bracelet should measure about 7½ inches (19 cm) in length.

9 To make the fly dangles on the bracelet, cut approximately 24 pieces of the 22-gauge gold-filled wire. Each piece should measure 1¼ inches (3.2 cm) in length.

BRAD WINTER
Necklace from the *Carnival Series*, 2002
Each element, 3 x 3 x ⅝ in. (7.6 x 7.6 x 1.6 cm)
Steel, paint, found sheet metal, roofing tin,
cookie tin; fabricated
Photo by Courtney Frisse

10 Use the following process to make and attach a fly dangle to each bracelet loop, starting with the second loop from the clasp. Follow steps 3 and 4 to make the wire loop. Before wrapping the ends of the loops, attach one end to the bracelet chain loop, then follow step 5 to wire wrap the end. Slip on a 2- to 3-mm glass bead and make a second loop (steps 3 add 4). Slip one of the flies on the wire and wrap the wire end. Repeat this step to attach a fly dangle to every open loop on the chain.

FOR THE EARRINGS

1 Following steps 8 and 9 of the bracelet instructions, make four beaded fly dangles, two for each earring, but do not attach the dangles to a chain.

2 Follow bracelet steps 3, 4, and 5 to make one beaded, looped link for each earring. Before wrapping the end of the wire on the second loop, slip on the two beaded fly dangles and wrap around the wire end.

3 Use pliers to open the loops on the ear wires. Attach one beaded chain to each ear-wire loop, then close loop to secure.

CHECK IT OUT

Probably the first written reference to fly-fishing is in Ælian's *Natural History,* authored in approximately 200 A.D. Ælian related a Macedonian method of catching fish, describing how the fishermen avoided using real flies as bait. (The human touch caused their wings to wilt and the insects to lose their natural color and, in turn, fish considered them unfit food.) Instead, Ælian explained, the Macedonians fastened crimson wool around a hook and attached to it two waxy colored feathers grown under a cock's wattles.

beach glass necklace

Use naturally frosted glass collected from the shore to enhance a stunning silver necklace.

Materials

Beach glass, approximately 20 pieces

Sterling silver round wire, 18 gauge, 3 to 5 feet
 (0.9 to 1.5 m)

Solder

Found, handmade, or purchased sterling silver chain
 in length of your choice, pictured necklace is
 18 inches (45.7 cm) long.

Sterling silver toggle clasp

Small jump rings for toggle clasp

Tools & Supplies

Safety goggles

Diamond drill bit, ⅟₁₆ inch (1.6 mm)

Flexible shaft

Diamond core bit, approximately ³⁄₁₆ inch (4.8 mm)

Mandrel for jump rings, approximately ⅜ inch (1 cm)
 in diameter

Jeweler's saw and saw blades

Soldering kit, see page 35

Chasing hammer

File

Flat-nose pliers, 2 pairs

Step by Step

1 Review the directions on page 40 for drilling
 glass. Put on a pair of safety goggles. Use the
⅟₁₆-inch (1.6 mm) diamond bit to drill through each
piece of beach or tumbled glass. Replace the bit in
the drill with the ³⁄₁₆-inch (4.8 mm) diamond core bit
and enlarge each hole.

2 Using the 18-gauge sterling silver round wire,
 create one jump ring for each piece of glass
you want to hang from the chain. The jump rings
created for this project are each approximately ⅜
inch (9.5 mm) in diameter. Saw them apart and set
them aside.

3 Lay the drilled beach glass in a row on your
 work surface. Select several glass shapes that
interest you. Replicate the outlines of these shapes
by bending pieces of 18-gauge sterling silver wire.
Solder the shapes closed. Use a hammer to slightly
flatten each soldered wire shape. Texture the shapes
with a file or hammer as desired.

4 Use one jump ring to hang each piece of drilled
 beach glass on the chain. Close each jump ring
tightly. Hang a soldered wire shape at random inter-
vals to harmonize with and accentuate the glass.

5 Attach the toggle clasp to the ends of the chain
 with small jump rings.

CHECK IT OUT

Beach glass can come from river, lake, sea, or ocean
shores. Generally, rougher glass comes from inland areas
where the water currents are less turbulent. Locations with
heavy surf create the smoothest forms. Beach glass is most
abundant in brown, green, and frosty clear, as those are
the most common bottle colors now
in use. Less often, one might find
glass in colors rarely used for
modern commercial containers:
red, lavender, blue, aqua,
and peach.

TRACK IT DOWN

• Get to know the places where you intend to collect.
 Determine the best areas and times of the year to do so,
 and pay attention to the tides so you can search when
 the water recedes.
• Use your collection of wave-tumbled glass gathered on
 seaside vacations to create this necklace, or easily simulate the look of beach glass by
 reusing broken wine or water bottles.
 Follow the directions on pages
 45 and 46 to tumble your
 own glass shards.

sea chart
pendant

Pay tribute to journeys taken by preserving mementos in a pendant. Use these same instructions to create a metal frame for other paper ephemera, such as photos, prints, drawings, or text.

Materials

Sterling silver sheet, 24 to 18 gauge

Found road map, topography map, boat chart, or other paper memento

Varnish or laminating paper (optional)

Glue

Miniature screws or bolts with nuts to fit

Large jump ring for bale

Tools & Supplies

Dividers or circle template and scribe

Jeweler's saw and saw blades

File

Sandpaper

Steel block

Center punch

Chasing hammer

Flexible shaft

Small drill bits

Needle

Plastic or heavy paper

Wire cutter

Scribe (optional)

Burr (optional)

Liver of sulfur (optional)

Step by Step

1 Using the dividers or the template, scribe two identical circles on the sterling silver sheet. Use the jeweler's saw to cut out the circles. File and sand the cut edges, making sure the circles remain exactly the same size.

2 Use the dividers or a smaller circle from the template and a scribe to draw a second circle inside one of the silver circles cut in step 1. Pierce and saw out the interior circle. File and sand the inside edge of this "frame."

3 Drill four matching holes through both silver circles at the 12-, 6-, 3-, and 9-o'clock positions. Make sure the holes in each circle line up exactly. Rotate the silver pieces so the drilled holes are in the 1-, 4-, 7-, and 10-o'clock positions.

4 Choose a section of the map (or other paper) to use, and cut it to fit the outside edge of the silver circles. If desired, you can laminate the map at this stage or you can varnish it after it has been glued in place. (Boat charts don't always need varnish as they are frequently printed on waterproof papers.) Glue the map to the solid silver circle, making sure the image is in the right position, and let dry. Use a needle to pierce the map where it covers the drilled holes.

5 Make a template from plastic or heavy paper that is the exact size of the inner circle of the silver frame and place it over the map. The template protects the image from damage when you handle the piece or if you have to polish or buff it.

6 Line up the holes in the silver frame with those in the solid back piece. Feed the miniature screws or bolts through the drilled holes and attach the nuts on the back of the piece, clamping the map in place. Be patient; the nuts are very small and your fingers may suddenly seem very large!

7 Use wire cutters to trim off the ends of the screws or bolts just above the nuts. If you do not have wire cutters, file or sand the ends above the tightened nuts. Gently tap the end of the screws or bolts to flatten them into the back of the nuts. (This process is similar to flaring a rivet and prevents the nut from unscrewing.)

sea chart
pendant

8 Drill a hole through the top of the pendant at the 12-o'clock position. Feed a large jump ring through this hole to be the pendant's bale.

9 If desired, you can now extend any lines (such as coastlines or road lines) off the map and onto the frame. Scribe the lines first, then use a small burr to engrave them. Blacken the engraved lines with a patina, such as liver of sulfur, if you wish. To do this, carefully paint the engraved lines, buff off any excess patina, and polish the frame with a cloth.

Variations

• You can make the metal frame pendant any shape you desire. The artist chose the round shape and brass hardware to reflect the nautical nature of the sea chart enclosure. If you were to frame a road map for instance, shapes that reflect a specific destination would be really interesting.

• If you make a wider frame, you could set stones in it to suggest a landscape or to simulate stars or traffic lights.

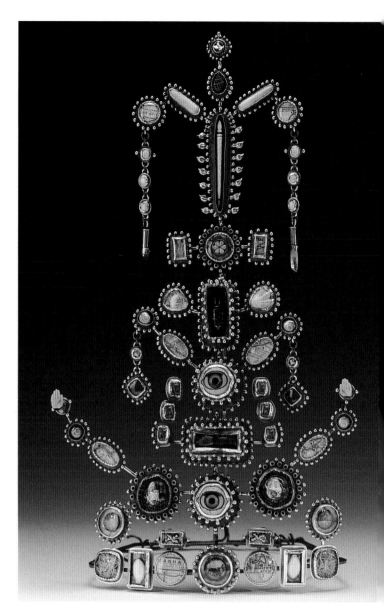

KRISTIN DIENER
Historic Reality Tiara, 2001
18 x 10 x 8 in. (45.7 x 25.4 x 20.3 cm)
Sterling silver, brass, 1979 road atlas, watch crystals, glass, bottle caps, votives, doll eyes, squash seeds from artist's great-grandmother, cottonwood beetle, guinea hen feathers, wisdom teeth, fingernail clippings, toothpick, gunshells; fabricated
Photo by Pat Berrett

hardware charm
bracelet

Nuts and bolts, keys and pulleys all have individual charm. Link them together with ease to fashion a super stylish bracelet.

hardware charm
bracelet

Materials
Assorted hardware, such as screws, electrical
     connectors, washers, and keys
Assorted fishing hardware, such as swivels,
     connectors, and lures (hooks removed)
Tin-coated copper wire, 18 gauge
16 to 20 safety snap swivels, size 18 or 20, brass,
     stainless, or black
Toggle clasp

Tools & Supplies
Flexible shaft or small handheld rotary tool (optional)
Small drill bits (optional)
Wire cutters
Chasing hammer
Needle-nose pliers
Pliers

Step by Step

1 Sort through the hardware and arrange it on
your work surface in an organized fashion. This
preparation will help you space similar pieces
throughout the bracelet. Assess which hardware
pieces have holes and can be used like a bead and
which ones need to be altered through drilling or
wiring in order to be connected to the bracelet.
Keep in mind that some pieces may not need head
pins and can be directly attached to the swivels on
the bracelet. Drill holes through the hardware components as needed.

2 Use the wire cutters to cut approximately 20
pieces of the 18-gauge wire, each 5 inches
(12.7 cm) long. Hammer one end of each wire piece
to create paddle-shaped head pins. Cut about 10
additional 5-inch (12.7 cm) pieces of the 18-gauge
wire, but do not hammer their ends.

3 Your bracelet connections will be unique to the
hardware you've selected. Often, you can handle the components as you would beads, stringing
and wire-wrapping them on head pins. Wrap the
wire with a bold flourish or with delicate consistency
or a combination of both—the choice is yours.
Thread one or more components on a hammered
wire head pin, then use the pliers to make a loop in
the wire. Hold the loop with the pliers, then take the
long end of the head pin and wrap it around the
bottom of the loop several times. Cut off any excess
wire close to the wrap. To avoid a sharp edge, use
the pliers to tightly press in the cut wire end.

4 To assemble the bracelet, open one swivel,
attach two components, and close the swivel.
Open a second swivel, attach one component,
connect the second swivel to the first one through
the small hole at the end, add a second component, and close the second swivel. Repeat this
procedure to complete a bracelet of the desired
length. Be sure to connect the swivels the same
way each time so the bracelet lays nicely and the
components hang consistently. The bracelets pictured on page 83 are each approximately 7 inches
(17.8 cm) long.

5 Add the toggle clasp to the ends of the
bracelet by attaching it on the last swivels.
To finish the bracelet, gently pinch each swivel
connection with pliers to secure the swivels and
keep them closed.

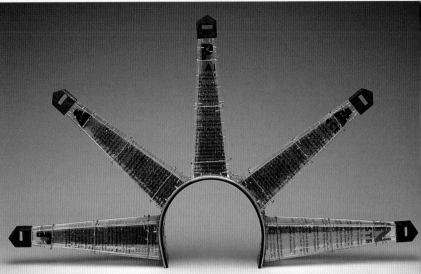

EMIKO OYE
Truth 4: The Past Is Present—Violations of the IV,
from the crown series *State of Liberty,* 2003
18¼ x 31 x 3 in. (46.4 x 78.7 x 7.6 cm)
Recycled thermoplastic sheet, recycled wood,
recycled plastic film, soil from Manzanar
Relocation Center, sterling silver, fine silver, steel
Photos by George Post

CHECK IT OUT

A safety snap swivel is a piece of fishing tackle used to attach a lure to a line. On one end, a wide loop opens like a safety pin to hold a lure. On the opposite end, the swivel mechanism allows the lure to pivot freely. Safety snap swivels come in many sizes and colors for use with different types of fish and fishing conditions.

"The birth of these bracelets is the result of being married to a sportsman and wandering through many an aisle filled with bright silvers, metals, brasses, and interesting shapes. Several years ago, as I aimlessly walked through the aisles, I remembered how when I was a kid, I'd made a swivel bracelet while sitting in a johnboat with my grandfather. Suddenly, the fishing department took on a new excitement, and it wasn't long before I was discovering other found objects with which to make my bracelets." MARY HETTMANSPERGER

TRACK IT DOWN

• Clean out your toolbox, tackle box, or junk drawer, and make the most of the intrinsic beauty of hardware by linking it up on a charming chain.

guitar pick
necklace

Guitar picks come in awesome colors and shapes. Assemble them with jump rings to form a necklace that rocks.

Materials

14 guitar picks, colors of your choice
Sterling silver sheet, 18 gauge
Sterling silver wire, 16 gauge
Commercial S clasp (optional)

Tools & Supplies

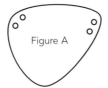

Figure A

Scribe
Jeweler's saw and saw blades
File
Sandpaper, 220 and 400 grit
Sanding mandrel
Flexible shaft
Drill bit, 0.8 mm
Steel block
Center punch
Chasing hammer
Round mandrel, 5 mm in diameter
Pliers

Step by Step

1 Use a scribe to trace one of the guitar picks onto the 18-gauge sterling silver sheet. Make sure to conserve space on the metal as you trace.

2 Use a jeweler's saw to saw out the silver guitar-pick shape, then use a file to smooth the cut edges. (The artist filed the metal at an angle to create a small bevel on the edges.) Sand the silver guitar pick with 220-grit sandpaper, then give it a final finish by rubbing it in circles with the 400-grit sandpaper.

3 Referring to figure A as a guide, use a scribe to mark the placement for the holes on each plastic guitar pick and the silver one. Drill these holes with a 0.8-mm bit. If the drilling causes any burrs on the silver guitar pick, sand them off with 400-grit sandpaper.

4 Use the scribe to draw a miniature guitar pick on a leftover plastic pick. (This small guitar pick hangs from the end of the necklace as an interesting decoration. The miniature pick shown is approximate-

ly one-third the size of a standard guitar pick.) Saw out this shape, and file its edges smooth. Use a 0.8-mm bit to drill a hole in the wide end of the miniature guitar pick.

5 Make 40 jump rings by wrapping the 16-gauge wire around a 5-mm mandrel and sawing the rings apart.

6 Create a clasp for the necklace by forming the 16-gauge wire into a closed S shape or use a commercial clasp if you prefer. Set the clasp aside.

7 Use the jump rings to connect all the guitar picks together, placing the silver pick somewhere in the middle of the chain and arranging the colors of the guitar picks as you like. To use one of the leftover jump rings to connect the clasp on one end of the chain, thread it through the two rings on the last guitar pick, then thread it through one side of the S clasp.

8 Connect the remaining jump rings to make a short chain. Thread the last jump ring on one end of the chain through the hole in the miniature silver guitar pick. Attach this chain to the two jump rings on the end of the necklace opposite the clasp. This chain makes a tail on the end of the necklace, allowing it to be worn at different lengths depending on where you hook the clasp.

CHECK IT OUT

Guitar picks come in many more styles than you might imagine. Custom-printed picks feature original, and often limited-edition, text and graph-ics. Guitar picks are even made from beautiful exotic woods such as rosewood and zebrawood, abalone shell, tortoise shell, and celluloid.

rock & roll
earrings

Give old 45-rpm records a new spin by sculpting the vinyl into dangle earrings.

Materials

Vinyl records

Sterling silver wire, 20 or 22 gauge

Tools & Supplies

Awl or other marking tool

Shape templates (optional)

Jeweler's saw and saw blades

File

Sandpaper, fine

Flexible shaft

Small drill bits

Wire cutters

Round-nose pliers

Chain-nose pliers

Step by Step

1 Design and mark four shapes on the vinyl records. (Draw the shapes freehand or use a template.) This design features one square and one oval per earring.

2 Use the jeweler's saw to cut out the marked vinyl shapes. (The jeweler's saw will slide through the vinyl like a knife through warm butter.)

3 Use a file and sandpaper to clean and refine the edges of the cut vinyl.

4 Select a drill bit that is slightly larger than the width of the sterling silver wire. Separate the vinyl pieces into two earring sets. Drill a hole in the top of the lower dangle shapes and through the center of the top shapes.

5 Cut two 8-inch (20.3 cm) lengths of the sterling silver wire. File or sand the ends of the wire smooth.

6 Use the round-nose pliers to form a loop approximately 3 inches (7.6 cm) in from one end of one piece of wire. Slip the lower vinyl shape onto the wire and onto the loop. Loosely wrap the long piece of wire around the short length for several turns.

7 Slip the second vinyl shape, the top element, onto the wire. Loosely wrap the longer wire end around the shorter one. Cut off the wire after several turns. Form an ear hook with the remaining length of wire.

8 Repeat steps 6 and 7 to create the second earring.

CHECK IT OUT

Vinyl didn't become the primary material in the manufacture of records until the 1960s. The standard disc comes in black, but it should be noted that a dye is added to achieve that color. Record manufacturers have also used colored vinyl, either clear or opaque, to attract buyers. A quick glance through a used record store might net anything from transparent violet to solid green. Occasionally, manufacturers added various colors in a speckled or swirled pattern. This splash vinyl, as it is called, is rare, usually the product of a press experiment, and record collectors willingly pay high prices for it. Picture discs, with a graphic layer sandwiched between the layers of vinyl, are also highly collectable. Although some predicted the CD would be the demise of vinyl records, the retro trend and DJs who spin electronic music have spurred a renewed interest in the format.

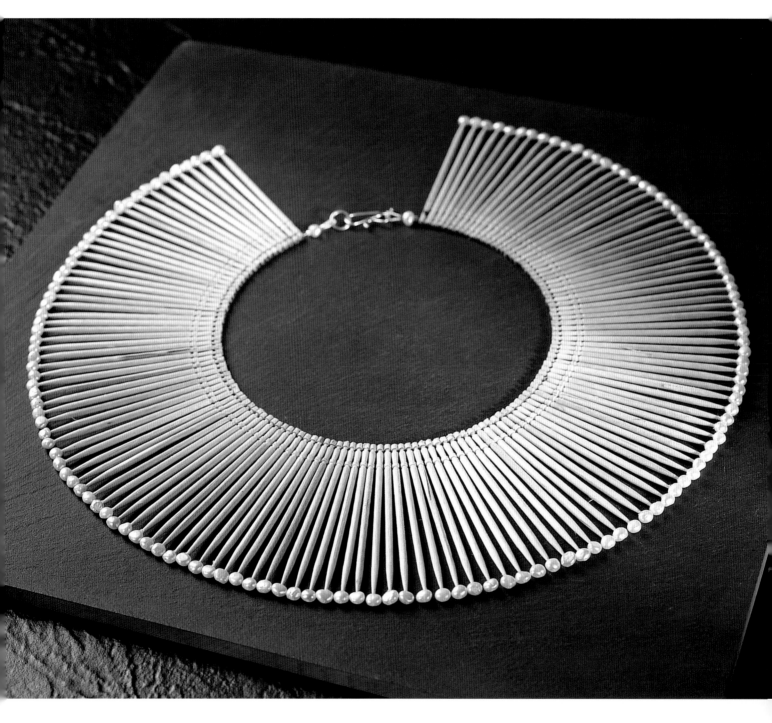

DESIGNER: **JOANNA GOLLBERG**

toothpick necklace

This necklace illustrates how the repetition of a simple, ordinary object leads to a composition of formal elegance.

Materials

Two-part epoxy
Freshwater pearls, 2 strands
Wooden toothpicks with turned ends
Tigertail beading wire
French wire, sterling silver or silver colored
4 crimp beads, sterling silver
Clasp and hook, handmade or commercial

Tools & Supplies

Flexible shaft
Drill bit, 0.5 mm
Snips
Chain-nose pliers

Step by Step

1 Follow the manufacturer's instructions to mix the two-part epoxy. Glue one freshwater pearl on the pointed end of each toothpick. (This necklace is 15 inches [38.1 cm] long and 140 toothpicks were used.) Let the glue dry.

2 Use the flexible shaft and the 0.5-mm bit to drill a hole in the top of each toothpick. Be sure to drill straight across, perpendicular to the length of the toothpick.

3 While the 0.5-mm bit is in the flexible shaft, drill a hole through two leftover pearls that are not glued onto toothpicks.

4 Use the snips to cut a length of the tigertail beading wire about 6 inches (15.2 cm) longer than the length of your necklace. This gives you lots of extra working space with the wire. Use the snips to cut two pieces of French wire, each about 10 mm long.

5 Thread a crimp bead, one of the drilled pearls, a second crimp bead, one piece of French wire, and half of the clasp onto the tigertail wire. Bend the French wire into a loop and rethread it through the crimp bead, the pearl, and the other crimp bead. Pull the tigertail wire tightly so the French wire is firmly in place. Use the chain-nose pliers to securely crimp the crimp beads. (The artist always uses two crimp beads at the ends of her necklaces. The extra crimp bead helps prevent the necklace from coming unstrung.) Use the snips to cut off any extra tigertail wire that protrudes from the last crimp bead.

6 Thread all of the drilled toothpicks onto the tigertail beading wire. Repeat step 5, using the other half of the clasp. Make sure all the toothpicks settle next to each other nicely, leaving no extra room on the necklace. Use the snips to cut off the extra tigertail wire.

CHECK IT OUT

According to recent experimental research, our early human ancestors may have known a thing or two about dental hygiene. Scientists who examined grooves left on fossilized teeth believe that some civilizations used grass stalks as toothpicks. The grooved teeth date back 1.8 million years. If these findings indeed mark the use of improvised toothpicks, this habit would be the oldest human custom yet recorded.

The popular use of toothpicks is well documented in the ancient cultures of China, Japan, India, Iran, and other eastern civilizations. Early humans made most toothpicks from fibrous sticks taken from trees, but other varieties were made from gold or bronze.

DESIGNER: ELIZABETH A. HAKE

knotted rubber
bracelet

Cover an out-of-fashion bangle or O-ring with a simple series of knots. The repeating knots pattern completely covers the bracelet, while the alternating knots pattern lets a little color peek through the rubber.

Materials

Bicycle tire rubber inner tube

Recycled bangle or O-ring bracelet, at least 3/16 inch (5 mm) thick (old glitter-filled bangles were used for this project)

Cyanoacrylate glue or other strong adhesive

Tools & Supplies

Ruler

Scissors

Roller-ball pen

Needle-nose pliers

Step by Step
ALTERNATING KNOT DESIGN
PREPARING THE RUBBER

1 Use the scissors to cut a section of the rubber inner tube that is 40 inches (1 m) long. Make sure the rubber doesn't have a valve stem or any rips or patches.

2 Cut lengthways along one of the inner tube seams to create one long rectangle of rubber.

3 Determine the top and bottom ends of the rubber rectangle. Measure 5/8 inch (1.6 cm) over from the left edge of the bottom end of the rectangle and mark this point with a roller-ball pen.

4 Place the scissors on the marked point and cut lengthways up the rubber. Cut the line as straight as possible, 5/8 inch (1.6 cm) inside and parallel to the left edge of the entire 40-inch (1 m) piece. Use the seams on the inner tube as a visual guide. Once you've cut the strip of rubber, wash it with soap and water, then dry it.

MAKING THE FIRST KNOT

5 Lay the bangle or O-ring bracelet (hereafter referred to as "the ring" for clarity) on the table in front of you. Imagine the ring is the face of a clock. Grab it in the 12-o'clock position with your thumb on the front of the ring (facing you) and your index finger on its back.

6 Place the left side of the bottom end of the rubber strip under your thumb on the front side of the ring. The free end of the strip should be angled up and to the right.

"I have been working with rubber since 1995, so I understand some of its capabilities and limitations. Having that in mind I try to approach the material with no preconceived ideas. I listen to what it wants to do, the way in which it wants to bend, and I go with it. When I have a promising design possibility, I work with the dimensions and variations until I refine that particular idea.

Ultimately, to me success is achieved when the final piece makes people exclaim, 'It's so intricate, so beautiful!' My work is achieved from society's debris, that which is cast off as no longer viable, in a word, trash. Taking something that is perceived as worthless and giving it a new life, making it desirable as adornment...now that is a beautiful feeling!" ELIZABETH A. HAKE

knotted rubber
bracelet

7 Slightly lift up the strip and grab it with your right thumb and index finger about 1 inch (2.5 cm) away from the point at which it is being held. Flip the strip back on itself, away from you, and over the top of the ring. Place the strip under your left index finger on the back of the ring and hold. You have created a loop over the ring. Pull the rest of the loose strip from the back of the ring up through the center of the ring and toward you.

8 Take the loose end of the strip and put it into the loop from your left-hand side, going behind the ring and coming out at the right side of the loop. While holding the knot with your left hand around the ring, pull the free end of the strip in a downward motion with your right hand. Adjust and gently pull the rubber until the knot is snug. If you pull too hard, the triangle will start to pull into itself and will not look as good.

MAKING THE SECOND KNOT

9 Grab the ring with your left thumb on the front and your index finger on the back. The strip should be laying behind the ring and directly to the right of the first knot. Grab the strip with your right thumb and index finger about 1 inch (2.5 cm) to the right of your left thumb and fold it toward you over the top of the ring. Place the strip under your left thumb and hold. You have made a loop that goes over the ring.

10 Pull the remainder of the loose strip through the center of the ring and away from you. Take the loose end of the strip and, from the back of the ring, feed it through the left-hand

side of the loop. The strip is now in front of the ring after exiting the bottom right side of the loop. While holding the knot around the ring with your left hand, pull the loose end of the strip in a downward motion with your right hand. Gently pull the strip and adjust the knot until it is snug.

11 Continue to make knots around the ring, repeating first the knot described in steps 6 through 8, then the knot described in steps 9 and 10. Knot the rubber until the right-hand edge of the last knot tied meets the left-hand side of the first knot tied.

FINISHING THE BRACELET

12 Make sure the knots are spaced the way you want them to be. Work your way around the whole bracelet, making every knot a little tighter or looser as needed. Pull any slackness out of the knotted rubber strip all the way to the loose end.

13 Undo the last tied knot. Cut the tail end of the strip under the first knot to ½ inch (1.3 cm) long. Following the manufacturer's instructions, use a small amount of cyanoacrylate or other adhesive to adhere the rubber to the ring. Let dry. Retie the last knot and cut the leftover rubber strip, leaving a tail end that is 3 inches (7.6 cm) long.

14 Use needle-nose pliers to insert the tail under the outside flap of the first knot. Feed the loose end of the last knot through the gap and pull snug.

ELIZABETH A. HAKE
Revolve, 1996
13 x 20 x 3 in. (33 x 50.8 x 7.6 cm)
Turntable pads, hubcaps, stainless screws
and nuts, cubic zirconia
Photo by David A. Hake

15 Place a dab of cyanoacrylate or other adhesive under the rubber end that has been tucked under the knot. Cut off any excess rubber tail that sticks out past the knot.

REPEATING KNOT DESIGN

1 Follow the instructions for the alternating knot design through step 8.

2 Grab the loose end and the ring directly to the right of the first knot. Pull the entire loose end of strip up through the center of the ring toward you. Wrap it snugly around the front of the ring, then grab it with your thumb and hold.

3 Grab the strip 1 inch (2.5 cm) away from your left thumb and make a loop by pulling the strip down behind the ring. Hold it there with your index finger. Pull the loose end up through the center of the ring to the front again. Feed the loose end of the strip into the top left-hand side of the loop and out the bottom right side of the loop. The strip is now behind the ring. Pull it snug.

4 Repeat steps 2 and 3 until you've tied knots all the way around the ring. To complete the bracelet, follow steps 12 through 15 of the alternating knot design.

DESIGNER: **LILLA LE VINE**

sew fine brooch

Make a gorgeous brooch with ease from scraps of fine fabric and trim.

Variation

Materials

Cardboard, 4 x 4-inch (10.2 x 10.2 cm) square

Cotton batting to cover cardboard

Velvet or background fabric of your choice

Glue

Lace

Dyes for lace (burgundy and green dyes were used for this project)

Thread to match background fabric

Metal leaves or other found metal object

Narrow ribbon, 8½ inches (21.6 cm) or enough for three gathered flowers

2 small oval beads to hang on the chain ends

Found silver chain, approximately 8½ inches (21.6 cm)

3 beaded dangles (the artist's were cut from a length of fringe)

Metal cone or other conical found object

Small glass bead

Seed beads to match other embellishments

Metal butterfly or other found object

Pin back

Felt, to cover back of brooch

Tools & Supplies

Scissors or craft knife

Sewing needle

Step by Step

1 Use scissors or a craft knife to cut the cardboard into an egg shape that is 3½ inches (8.9 cm) long. Cover the cardboard with the batting. Position the velvet or other fabric over the batting, wrap it around the cardboard form, and glue it on the back. Turn the brooch's fabric-covered base form so the narrow end points downward.

2 Following the manufacturer's instructions, dye the lace the color of your choice and let dry. Position the lace on one side of the base form. Use the needle and thread to stitch the dyed lace onto the fabric.

3 Place the metal leaves or other found objects about halfway down the base form, on the opposite side of the lace. Sew the objects to the fabric.

4 Cut the narrow ribbon into three equal lengths and gather each length to make a rose. Stitch the roses onto the lace and/or onto the background fabric.

5 Sew one oval bead on each end of the found chain. Place a dab of glue on the end of each knot to strengthen it.

6 To make the tassel, restring the beaded dangles on doubled thread. Roll the top of the thread and glue it to secure. Fold the found chain so one end hangs a little longer than the other. Sew and glue the folded chain to the top of the metal cone or other conical found object. Use a needle and thread to pull the beaded tassels up into the cone. Knot the thread and add a drop of glue to secure. Thread one glass bead onto the top of the cone. Sew the completed tassel to the background fabric.

7 Use a needle and thread to sew seed beads on the lace and around the perimeter of the background fabric. Sew the found metal butterfly or other found object in place to complete the composition.

8 Sew the pin back to the felt piece. Neatly adhere the felt to the back of the brooch with glue and let dry. Trim the edges of the felt to complement the shape of the brooch.

"All of the objects that inspired this brooch came from a broken jewelry box; a filigree butterfly (a bit bent and rusted), three silver leaves, and a silvery cone that immediately spoke 'tassel top' to me. I cleaned everything and gave them a wash of green and gold paint, leaving most of the original color." LILLA LE VINE

spoons & spinners
charm bracelet

Fish aren't the only creatures that will be attracted to this a-luring collection of found metal spoons and beads.

Materials

Found spoons and spinners,
   approximately 9
Gold-filled wire, 20 gauge, 6 feet (1.8 m)
Found glass beads, 6 to 7 mm,
   approximately 10
Gold-plated toggle clasp
Found glass beads, 3 to 4 mm,
   approximately 9

Tools & Supplies

Flush wire cutters
Pumice
Chain-nose pliers
Round-nose pliers

Step by Step

1 Use the flush wire cutters to remove the hooks from the spoons and spinners. Clean the surface of the spoons and spinners. Lightly rub the surface with pumice if desired, but be careful—if you use too much pressure, the applied decorations may rub off.

MAKING THE BEADED BRACELET

2 Cut approximately 10 pieces of the gold-filled wire to make the 6½-inch (16.5 cm) bracelet chain. Each piece should be about 2¼ inches (5.7 cm) long.

3 Use the chain-nose pliers to make a right angle close to the center of one cut wire length.

4 With the round-nose pliers, grasp the wire at its right angle bend. With your other hand, wrap the wire around the top of the pliers to make a loop.

5 Use the chain-nose pliers to lightly grasp the loop on either side. With your other hand, wrap the wire around the neck of the loop about two to three times.

When wrapping the wire around, pull it tight. Cut off excess wire with the flush cutters.

6 Thread a 6- to 7-mm bead onto the wire and make another right angle, leaving a little room above the bead for wrapping the other wire end. Repeat steps 4 and 5 to complete the loop. Adjust both finished loops so they are facing the same direction.

7 Repeat steps 3 and 4 with a second piece of wire to make another beaded link, but before wire wrapping the end, slip the new loop through the first completed loop. Continue making the second link as described in steps 5 and 6. Repeat this step until you have a beaded chain that measures 6½ inches (16.5 cm) in length. Attach the toggle clasp to the beaded chain. Adjust the loops before wrapping the ends so the clasp moves freely. The bracelet should measure about 7¾ inches (19.7 cm) in length.

MAKING THE SPOON & SPINNER DANGLES

8 Cut approximately nine pieces of the 20-gauge wire, each 2 inches (5 cm) in length.

9 Starting with the second loop from the clasp, make one spoon or spinner dangle to be attached to a loop in between each beaded link. Follow steps 3 and 4 to make a wire loop. Before wrapping the ends of the loops, attach one end to the bracelet chain loop, then follow step 5. Slip on a 3- to 4-mm glass bead and make a loop (again following steps 3 and 4). Before wrapping the end of the wire, slide one spoon or spinner onto the loop. Repeat this step until there is a spoon or spinner dangle between each beaded loop, varying the sizes and shapes of the spoons and spinners for visual interest.

energy talisman

Harness the energy of found objects and channel it into an evocative necklace.

Materials

Pencil stubs and colored pencil stubs

Plain or printed sheets of tissue paper, each
  8½ x 11 inches (21.6 x 27.9 cm)

Matte acrylic medium

Sterling silver bezel wire

Solder

Sterling silver sheet, 28 gauge or thinner

Sterling silver wire

Epoxy

Handmade, recycled, or purchased chain

Tools & Supplies

Jeweler's saw and saw blades

Sandpaper

Scissors

Typewriter (optional)

Paintbrush

Waxed paper

Soldering kit, see page 35

File

Knitting needle

Pliers

Wire cutter

Step by Step

1 Shorten pencils to desired lengths as needed, varying the lengths of the stubs. Lightly sand each pencil stub to create random worn surfaces.

2 Wrap a piece of scrap paper around one pencil stub to create a template. Mark the edge of the paper and unwrap. This will give you a close approximation of the material needed to wrap most of the pencils. Cut out a paper rectangle as long as the longest pencil stub.

3 Type text onto the tissue papers or use commercial tissue printed with text. Use the paper template to cut the tissue into rectangles.

4 Trim a tissue rectangle to fit one pencil stub. Brush the pencil with a thin coating of matte acrylic medium and wrap the tissue around the pencil. Smooth the tissue on the pencil surface and give the pencil an additional coat of acrylic medium. Set the pencil on a length of waxed paper to dry. Repeat this step to cover all the pencil stubs.

5 Use the jeweler's saw to remove the erasers from most of the pencil stubs. Saw the points from the remaining pencils, leaving the erasers intact.

6 Create a simple bezel out of sterling silver bezel wire to fit on the flat end of each stub. Solder the ends of each bezel. Solder one end of each bezel onto a piece of sterling silver sheet. Saw out the bezel cap. File and sand each bezel cap.

7 Using the knitting needle as a mandrel, wrap it with sterling silver wire to create a coil. Remove the coil and saw it to create jump rings.

8 Solder a jump ring to the top of each bezel cap, positioning the ring so the saw line is on the top. Secure one completed bezel cap to each pencil stub with a dab of epoxy.

9 Create a handmade chain and findings, or use a purchased chain and findings. Hang each of the pencil stubs from the chain, securing each with a jump ring.

"This piece was created to be a very powerful energy talisman. It is based on the same principles of the talismans created and worn in West Africa and Southeast Asia. Hunters and medicine healers wore teeth or bone of a specific animal for the powers that the animal held.

Energy Talisman is a collection of worn pencil stubs that a second grade class saved for me. I watched all the children hard at work thinking, writing, and erasing. I thought it would be amazing to contain that energy in these pencil stubs. Hence, the idea for Energy Talisman was born. This piece represents the energies the children put into the pencils stubs. It is a piece to be worn for invigoration and stimulation. I typed poetry on the same theme and used a transfer technique to apply it to the pencil stubs." SUSAN LENART KAZMER

river stone pin

A sleek stickpin makes a handsome mount for any found object. Here's an easy way to make your own.

Materials

River stone, approximately 1 x 1 inch (2.5 x 2.5 cm)

Sterling silver sheet, 20 gauge

Sterling silver tube, approximately ⅛ inch (3 mm) inside diameter

Sterling silver wire, 16 gauge

Solder

Small sterling silver tube

Tools & Supplies

Diamond twist drill bit, approximately ⅛ inch (3 mm)

Flexible shaft

Jeweler's saw and saw blades

Dividers or compass

Flat file

Steel block

Center punch

Chasing hammer

Small drill bits

Sandpaper

Soldering kit, see page 35

Chain-nose pliers

Pliers

Flaring tool

Polishing compound (optional)

Step by Step

1 Insert the diamond twist drill bit into the flexible shaft. Slowly and carefully drill the river stone from the front to the back.

2 Use the jeweler's saw to cut a disk that is approximately ¼ inch (6 mm) in diameter out of the 20-gauge sterling silver sheet. Drill a hole that is the same diameter as the tubing in the center of the disk.

3 Use the jeweler's saw to cut a piece of the sterling silver tubing to solder to the disk. The tubing must be long enough to pass through the river stone and stand approximately 2 mm above it.

4 Cut a piece of the 16-gauge sterling silver wire approximately 2½ to 3 inches (6.4 to 7.6 cm) long to use for the pin stem. Use a file to taper one end of the wire to a sharp point. Sand and polish the pin stem.

5 Use the flexible shaft to drill a hole the same diameter as the untapered end of the pin stem into the silver disk. Position this second hole in the disk under the hole for tubing.

6 Clean the disk, pin stem, and the tube for soldering. Flux both holes in the disk. Place the tube in its hole and flush with the back of the disk. Place the pin stem in its hole. Solder these elements with hard solder. Pickle and rinse the metal.

7 Hold the base of the pin stem with a pair of chain-nose pliers in one hand and a second pair of pliers in the other hand. Working your way down the pin stem to the point, use the pliers to twist the wire half a turn, then twist it back. This work hardens the pin stem and makes it stiff.

8 Grab the pin stem at its base with the chain-nose pliers. Use your other hand to bend the pin stem straight down to a 90-degree angle from the disk.

river stone pin

9 Select a piece of sterling silver tubing that is slightly larger in diameter than the point of the pin to use as a safety. Make sure the tubing will slide onto and approximately ¼ inch (6 mm) up the pin stem.

10 Use the soldering torch to fuse a small piece of scrap sterling silver into a ball. Solder the ball onto the end of the tube with hard solder. Pickle and rinse the safety. (If the safety does not fit the tapered pin stem snugly enough, slightly crimp the safety with a pair of pliers.)

11 Slide the river stone onto the tube setting. While supporting the back of the disk on a steel block, use a hammer and flaring tool to flare the end of the tubing. Rivet the stone in place. Clean and polish the tube rivet and stone as desired.

CHECK IT OUT

River stones are naturally polished, smooth pebbles found along the shores of rivers and beaches. The stones are slowly eroded by water pressure and the friction created by passing debris. They are thought to contain healing and magical properties; some believe them to be symbols of accelerated change. River stones are *en vogue* with massage therapists, who heat them for use in hot stone therapy. This centuries-old technique provides relief and relaxation for stressed bodies.

AARON MACSAI
Captured Spirits, 2001
2½ x 1¼ in. (6.4 x 3.2 cm)
Found arrowheads, 18-karat yellow gold, 18-karat white gold, coin, 14-karat gold; fabricated
Photo by artist

"I usually collect stones when I am fishing in various local streams. I have been collecting river stones and making jewelry with them since the early 1990s. When I look for stones I look for striking characteristics such as colors, stripes, and shapes. Each stone that I use is attractive all by itself. I do what I can to compliment it in some way by making jewelry and art." JASON JANOW

spork collar & earrings

Convert disposable cutlery into a tasteful necklace and earring set.

spork
collar & earrings

The Collar
Materials
Vintage wooden picnic utensils
Wood glue
Waxed linen thread
Small wooden beads
Bone ring

Tools & Supplies
Clamps
Small drill bits
Flexible shaft
Scissors
2 tapestry needles
Craft knife or jeweler's saw and saw blades

Step by Step

1 Spread a thin coat of wood glue along the handle of one utensil. Adhere a second utensil facing the first. Clamp them together to ensure a good bond and let dry. Glue together as many pairs of utensils as you think you will need. This collar was created with 24 utensil pairs.

2 Choose a drill bit that is slightly larger than the diameter of the waxed linen thread. Measure ¼ inch (6 mm) down from the end of the handle of an extra, single utensil. Drill a centered hole at this point. Measure ½ inch (1.3 cm) down from the first hole and drill a second centered hole. You will use this utensil as a template to ensure accurate placement for the holes drilled in the glued utensils.

3 Use the template made in step 2 to mark the hole placement for each glued utensil pair. Drill two holes in each pair.

4 Cut four 36-inch (0.9 m) lengths of the waxed linen thread. Thread two tapestry needles (or two needles that fit through the drilled holes), each

with one length of thread. Set the unused threads aside. Loosely knot the two lengths of thread together approximately 12 inches (30.5 cm) from one end.

5 Thread a small wooden bead onto one needle, then thread the needle through the top hole of one utensil.

6 Bring the second needle up from behind the utensil and thread it up through the top hole in the handle and the bead. You've made one stitch. Pull the knot against the utensil.

7 Repeat the sequence described in steps 5 and 6 until you've linked all utensils through their top holes. Loosely knot the thread ends after the last utensil.

8 Thread the needles with the two remaining thread lengths. Repeat the process described in steps 5 through 7 to sew and bead the second row of holes.

9 Once both rows are sewn together, begin to tighten the thread and make the spoons lay flat against each other. Do this by placing the collar on a flat surface and tightening each stitch one by one.

10 On one end of the collar, tie square knots using two threads as carrier threads and the other two threads as knotting threads (see figure A). Knot about 1½ inches (3.8 cm) of the thread using this macramé technique.

Figure A

11 Attach a bone ring to the knotted thread by looping the threads to capture the ring, then make one or two square knots on top of the knotted strand.

12 Thread a needle with one of the threads. Slip the needle through the knotted strand, running it along the carrier threads. Trim the thread. Repeat with a second thread.

13 Use a craft knife or jeweler's saw to cut out a small rectangle from the handle of a leftover utensil. Drill a hole in the center of the rectangle.

14 Tie square knots with the loose threads at the opposite end of the collar. Work approximately 1½ inches (3.8 cm), then thread the two threads through the hole in the wooden rectangle. Bring the threads back around and continue knotting them down the knotted strand. Finish the thread ends as described in step 12.

The Earrings
Materials
4 vintage wooden picnic utensils
Wood glue
Sterling silver wire, 20 or 22 gauge,
  approximately 8 inches (20.3 cm)
4 small wooden beads

Tools & Supplies
Craft knife or jeweler's saw and saw blades
File or sandpaper
Clamps
Small drill bits
Flexible shaft
Round-nose pliers

Step by Step

1 Use a craft knife or jeweler's saw to cut the handles of four wooden utensils to short, equal lengths. File or sand the cut ends as needed.

2 Spread a thin coat of wood glue along the handle of one utensil. Adhere a second utensil facing the first. Clamp them together to ensure a good bond and let dry. Repeat to make a second pair.

3 Select a drill bit through which the sterling silver wire will easily pass. Drill a single centered hole close to the end of each of the glued utensil pairs.

4 Cut two pieces of sterling silver wire, each approximately 4 inches (10.2 cm) long. File the ends of the wire smooth.

5 Measure halfway up from the end of one wire and make a loop. Slip one pair of glued and drilled utensils and two beads on the wire. Wrap one end of the wire tightly around the other end. Trim excess wire. Repeat this step to create the second bead and utensil dangle. Form the ear wires as desired.

ROBLY A. GLOVER
Lure/Allure, 2003
24 x 24 x ½ in. (61 x 61 x 1.3 cm)
Sterling silver, silicone
Photo by artist

show-me-the-money
bangles & dangles

Convert printed metal into jewelry that reflects your good cents.

The Bracelet
Materials

Sterling silver tubing, to snugly fit into the holes in the metal signs

Letters or symbols from found metal signs (with prepunched, centered holes if possible)

Tools & Supplies

Jeweler's saw and saw blades

Files

Sandpaper

Steel block

Flaring tool

Riveting hammer

Center punch

Flexible shaft and drill bits or hole punch for metal

Bracelet mandrel or other large dowel such as rolling pin or PVC pipe

Step by Step

1 Use the jeweler's saw to cut the sterling silver tubing into short lengths, three for each end of each metal letter or symbol. Each tube needs to be a suitable length for riveting two metal letters or symbols together. File or sand the tubing ends smooth.

2 If the letters or symbols you're using have prepunched and centered holes, rivet six of them together with the short lengths of tubing. If the found metal pieces don't have holes, punch or drill one in the center of each end, then rivet them together.

3 Find and mark the center point between one rivet made in step 2 and one edge of the metal. Drill or punch a hole at this point. Insert a tube into the hole, flare the tube, and rivet it. Repeat this process on the opposite side of the center rivet. You now have three tube rivets connecting one end of two found metal pieces.

4 Continue to drill or punch the metal and set the rivets as described in step 3 until all metal signs connect into a long band.

5 The last group of rivets will join the two ends of the bracelet. Tip: Here's a trick for setting these last three rivets. Flare one end of each tube before setting them. To join the two ends, bring them together and insert one tube through the center holes with its flared end on the inside of the bracelet. Slip the band onto a bracelet mandrel or large dowel. The flared end will prevent the tube rivet from slipping off as you begin to work. Flare the other end of the center rivet, then hammer alternately on each end of the rivet to set it as usual. Repeat this process to set the two remaining tube rivets.

"I found the $ and ¢ signs in the discontinued bin of a real hardware store—definitely not a typical big-box emporium. Centered holes at either end of each aluminum rectangle led me to believe they were once a part of an outmoded (if not archaic) signage system. Alas, only a very few letters were in the bin. I purchased each and every one of them and am hoarding them for future projects. If you find something interesting, buy it. It won't be there when you return (and really need the item)!" TERRY TAYLOR

bangles & dangles

The Earrings
Additional Materials
2 lengths of sterling silver wire, 20 gauge,
 6 inches (15.2 cm) each
2 sterling silver beads

Additional Tools & Supplies
Round-nose pliers
Chain- or flat-nose pliers
Flush cutters
Wood dowel, ½ inch (1.3 cm) in diameter

1 Use the round-nose pliers to form a loop approximately 2 inches (5 cm) in from one end of one
20-gauge silver wire piece.

2 Slip a letter or symbol from a found metal sign
onto the loop. String a sterling bead onto the
wire until it is snug against the loop.

3 Using the chain- or flat-nose pliers, wind the
shorter wire end around the longer end three or
four times. Cut off the excess wire and file the end
as needed to make it smooth.

4 Bend a right angle in the wire just above the
wrapped wire. Form an ear wire using the wood-
en dowel as a mandrel. Cut the end of the wire as
needed. Finish and smooth the end of the wire with
a file and sandpaper.

tin-tastic
bangle

Create this variation
with colorful, print-
ed metal from
recycled containers.

1 Use metal shears or a jeweler's saw to cut small
rectangles from recycled metal cans or containers. The size of the rectangles can be consistent or
varied depending upon the style you want to
achieve. (This project uses five rectangles, each 1 x
1¾ inches [2.5 x 4.4 cm] and one larger rectangle,
2¾ x 1¼ inches [7 x 3.2 cm].) File the cut metal
edges smooth.

2 To assemble the bracelet, follow the steps out-
lined for the Show-Me-the-Money Bangle with
one exception. Because there isn't a centered, prepunched hole on the metal rectangles, use two
equally spaced tube rivets rather than three to join
the band.

TRACK IT DOWN

• Preprinted containers
have grown increasingly
hard to find—most of
today's products are
packaged with paper
labels—but scan
international food
aisles or local ethnic
groceries, and you're sure to find
plenty of intriguing options.

• Put the word on the street that you're collecting preprinted
tin containers, and you're sure to receive more than you
bargained for from friends, family, and neighbors.

• If you're not above rummaging through recycling bins,
hang around restaurants on recycling night. You can usually
find stockpiles of olive oil tins, beer cans, and more!

tintype necklace

Use a vintage photograph with contrasting found objects to create a poetic piece of jewelry.

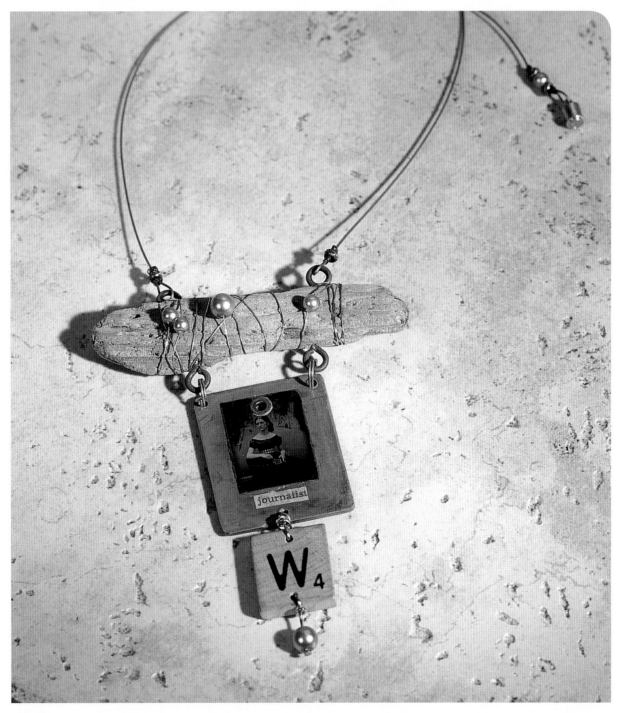

tintype
necklace

Materials

Brass or copper sheet, 18 gauge

Found piece of driftwood, wood, or branch

Gold or silver wire, thin

Assorted beads or pearls

4 screw eyes, small

Fast-drying epoxy

Gem tintype photo or laser-copied image*

Grommet (optional)

White glue

Printed text

2 head pins, each 2 inches (5 cm) long

Letter tile from word game

2 split rings

Acrylic paint (optional)

Multistrand, nylon-coated stainless
   steel beading cable**

4 to 8 crimp beads

Magnetic clasp

Clear paste wax

Tools & Supplies

Jeweler's saw and saw blades

Sandpaper

Steel block

Center punch

Hammer

Flexible shaft

Small drill bits

Scissors

Paintbrush

Needle-nose pliers

* A gem tintype is distinguished by its very small image size.
A laser-copied image will work just as well as an authentic
gem tintype for this project because the inks will not run
when they get wet.
** This type of cable is strong and flexible. Because it has a
nylon coating, it will not catch on clothing or poke your skin.

Step by Step

1 Use the jeweler's saw to cut a 1½ x 1¼-inch (3.8 x
3.2 cm) rectangle from the 18-gauge brass or copper sheet. Smooth the cut edges with sandpaper.
Dimple, then drill one hole near each corner of one of
the shorter ends of the metal rectangle. These two
holes will be used to hang the pendant. Drill a third
hole at the opposite end of the rectangle, centered
and near the edge.

2 Prepare the driftwood for adornment. Take a
moment to look at the wood and decide what
would look interesting. Wrap some wire around the
wood and add beads or faux pearls if desired. Thread
the four screw eyes into the wood; two on the top
edge and two on the bottom. Space the bottom
screw eyes at the same distance as the two holes in
the top of the metal rectangle.

3 Follow the manufacturer's directions to mix the
fast-drying epoxy. Adhere the gem tintype to the
brass rectangle with the epoxy. (This glue does not
dry immediately, so do not walk away and expect the
photo to remain in the correct position. Sometimes it
can slip or move, so keep a careful watch over it.)
After the epoxy is dry, drill a small hole through the
image and metal and add a decorative grommet if
desired. (If you are using a laser-copied image, attach
it to the metal with white glue. Add a little water to
the glue if it seems too thick.)

4 Select some interesting text from an old newspa-
per or book and cut it to fit on the metal under
the tintype. Attach the text clipping to the metal with
white glue.

5 Carefully drill a centered hole near the top and bottom edges of the word game tile. These small tiles
can sometimes be tricky to pierce, so take your time
making the hole. (Having a sharp drill bit will help.)

6 Place a fancy bead or two onto a head pin and thread it through the bottom hole of the word game tile. Wrap the rest of the head-pin wire around itself. (If the bead is large enough, you can hide the end of the wire inside the hole of the bead.) Snip off any excess wire.

7 Snip off the head on the second head pin. Feed the wire into the hole at the top of the game tile and loop it around itself. Feed the remaining head-pin wire through the hole at the bottom of the metal pendant and loop to secure. Snip off any excess wire.

8 Use pliers to feed one split ring through each of the holes at the top of the metal pendant. Once connected, use pliers to attach the split rings on the pendant to the screw eyes on the bottom of the driftwood (one ring per eye). This may take some maneuvering, so be patient.

9 Touch up areas or add highlights to the pendant with various colors of acrylic paint if desired. (The artist likes to use old-gold metallic paint.)

10 Measure a length of the nylon-coated stainless steel beading cable to use for each side of the pendant, then add about 1 inch (2.5 cm) extra for looping and connecting. (The necklace pictured has 9 inches [22.9 cm] of cable on each side, so two 10-inch [25.4 cm] pieces were cut.) Use snips to cut the cables to this length.

11 Thread one wire through one screw eye on the top edge of the driftwood. Slip a crimp bead on the wire. Once the bead is through the screw eye, make a loop in the wire and push the crimp bead over both pieces of wire. The shorter, salvage end of the wire should barely stick out of the bead. Compress the crimp bead with pliers to lock it in place.

12 String another type of fancy bead on the wire. Hide any excess salvage wire that extends past the crimp bead inside the hole of the fancy bead. String another crimp bead onto the wire to lock the fancy bead in place. Compress the crimp bead with pliers to secure it.

13 Repeat steps 11 and 12 at the opposite end of the first wire, but instead of looping the wire through the screw eye, loop it through one element of the magnetic clasp. String more fancy beads between the crimp beads at this end if desired.

14 Repeat steps 11 through 13 to attach the second wire to the second screw eye, adding crimp beads, fancy beads, and the clasp as described.

15 Use a paper towel to apply a thin covering of clear paste wax over the surface of the brass. Do not rub the surface too hard. You can cover the tintype if you like, but proceed slowly and gently.

fur love brooches

Refashion a neglected hand-me-down into a
unique piece of jewelry you'll be honored to wear.

Materials

Sterling silver sheet

Pin back

Solder

Two-part epoxy or other strong adhesive

Gold or silver wire for rivets

Recycled fur

Single post earring (optional)

Tools & Supplies

Jeweler's saw and saw blades

Files

Sandpaper

Dividers

Steel block

Center punch

Chasing hammer

Flexible shaft

Small drill bits

Soldering kit, see page 35

Small burr (optional)

Straight pin or needle

Leather scrap

Step by Step

1 Design and scribe two identical heart shapes on the sterling silver sheet. Use the jeweler's saw to cut out the hearts. File and sand the edges of the two metal hearts so they are exactly the same size.

2 Use dividers to scribe a smaller heart shape inside one of the metal pieces cut in step 1. (The area between the edge of the large heart and the scribed line should be wide enough to support rivets.) Pierce and saw out this interior shape. File and sand the inner edges. You now have a solid heart and a heart frame.

3 Solder the pin back onto the back side of the solid heart. Pickle and clean the metal.

4 Cut six pieces of the rivet wire, each approximately ¾ inch (1.9 cm) long. Ball one end of each rivet wire by holding it in the hot flame of a soldering torch.

5 Measure and mark six holes (or more if desired) evenly around the heart frame and the solid heart. These holes must line up exactly. (Take care to avoid marking holes that are too close to the pin back.) Dimple and drill holes at the marked points using a bit that is the same diameter as the rivet wire.

"I used furs recycled from old coats and collars for this project. This way I feel that the animal is remembered and not just thrown away. Any fur or faux fur fabric can be used. You can also use other fabric—I have used silk, velvets, and patchwork. These look wonderful stuffed with a little padding so the heart shape puffs out. Adding the earring is a great way to use a leftover when you loose one." GAE WEBSTER

fur love
brooches

ROBERT W. EBENDORF
Necklace, 2002
Pendant, 6 in. (15.2 cm) long
Coat-hanger wire, jawbone,
teeth, pearl, iron wire
Photo by Tim Lazure
Collection of A. Braun

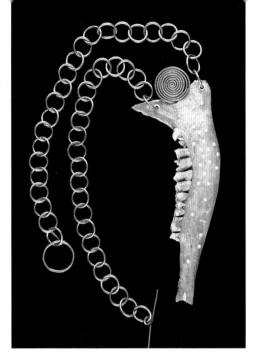

6 Optional: If you have a small burr, you may wish to slightly burr the back side of the holes in the solid heart. This way, the rivet heads will flatten into the hollows and be flush with the sheet metal. If you do not have a burr, you'll be able to feel the slightly raised rivets on the finished brooch.

7 Cut the recycled fur to fit the solid silver heart. Following the manufacturer's instructions, use the two-part epoxy or other strong-bonding glue to adhere the fur to the solid heart. If the fur is very long, you may need to trim it where the frame will sit, or you can comb it out to the sides so the lengths of fur fan out around the outside edge of the frame (see project photo, page 114, right brooch).

8 Place the heart frame over the fur-covered solid heart and use a straight pin to line up the drilled holes. (You may need to use a needle to pierce the leather under the fur.) Feed one rivet through one set of matching holes and the fur in between them. The balled side of the rivet should be on the front side of the brooch. Place a piece of leather on top of a steel block. Place the brooch on the block with the front side facing the leather to protect the silver and the wire rivets.

9 Trim the rivet wire to just above the back side of the brooch. Using a small hammer, lightly tap the end of the rivet wire to flare it. (If you burred the holes as described in step 6, the wires will flatten into the cups). Hint: If the wire bends over when hammered, it was probably too long. To correct this, straighten the wire, trim it a little more, and re-hammer the rivet.

10 Directly across from the brooch's first rivet, repeat steps 8 and 9 to make a second rivet. (Joining the holes that are opposite the first pair evenly pulls down and clamps shut the piece.) Repeat this process to rivet the remaining holes, always working with opposite pairs. Lightly sand any sharp rivets.

11 If you want to embellish the brooch with a recycled post earring, do so now. Select a drill bit that is the same diameter as the earring post. Carefully drill a hole through the fur and solid silver heart without damaging the pin back. Feed the earring post through the drilled hole and trim the post wire as if it were a rivet. Place a piece of leather on top of the steel block to protect the earring. Very gently and carefully hammer the end of wire until it flares.

Variation

To turn this project into a pendant, either solder a jump ring at the top of the heart or drill a hole and suspend it.

TRACK IT DOWN

- Look for old coats with fur collars, battered vintage muffs, or worn-out gloves with fur linings to reuse.
- Out-grown stuffed animals are a great source of fuzzy fur.

the performer **necklace**

The Performer is a two-part necklace joined by a lock and key. Placing different tassel constructions on different keys that fit the same lock change the figure's attire and her personality.

the performer necklace

Materials

FOR THE NECKLACE

Sterling silver wire, heavy gauge

Lock, such as a padlock or bike lock, with two or more keys

Steel or iron wire, assorted gauges

Typewriter ribbon spool or sewing machine bobbin

Assorted gears and washers

Assorted springs

Beads

Ribbons

Decorative threads

Translucent polymer clay or small doll head

FOR THE TASSEL OR GOWN

The materials you hang from the key depend on the style of the tassel or gown you wish to create. Here are some objects the artist used to realize her visions: gears, sewing bobbin, wire, ribbon, threads, beads, springs, chain, grommets, gears, typewriter ribbon holder, nuts, washers, screws, paper, cassette tape ribbon, tiny bells, television dial.

Tools & Supplies

Chopstick or knitting needle

Pliers

Wire cutters

Soldering kit, see page 35 (optional)

Step by Step

FORMING THE TORSO

1 If you've chosen a traditional padlock, cut a 12-inch (30.5 cm) length of thin wire. Fold the wire in half and slip the lock onto the folded wire.

2 Select a heavy-gauge wire to form the torso shape for the figure. Use pliers to coil a length of the wire into a flat spiral. Pull out the spiral to form a cone shape. Slip the cone shape onto the wire and lock. If needed, secure the cone shape to the wire with thin wire.

3 String spools, washers, beads, or other found objects onto the thin wire that holds the lock and torso shape. Set the assembly aside.

CREATING & ATTACHING THE HEAD & ARMS

4 Wind a wire coil around a chopstick or knitting needle. The coil needs to be at least 1 inch (2.5 cm) in length. Sculpt a head for the figure with the polymer clay. Form the figure's neck around the wire coil, leaving a bit of the coil exposed. Bake the polymer clay following the manufacturer's instructions. Alternately, you could use a small doll head rather than creating one from polymer clay.

5 Cut a 12-inch (30.5 cm) length of heavy wire and mark its center. Use round-nose pliers to create a single loop in the center of the wire. Pick up the lock and torso assembly. Slip the thin wire at the top of the assembly through the single loop in the heavy wire. Wrap the thin wire once or twice around the loop to secure it. Then attach the thin wire to the wire coil at the base of the polymer clay or doll head. Wrap the wire as tightly as possible to stabilize the head.

6 Slip beads, springs, ribbon, or other found embellishments onto each end of the heavy wire and secure. Set this assembly to the side.

CONSTRUCTING THE NECKPIECE

7 Cut a 15-inch (38.1 cm) length of the sterling silver wire. File the ends of the wire smooth. If you have a soldering torch, ball up each end of the sterling silver wire. Slip springs, beads, washers, and nuts onto the neck wire as desired. Use pliers to fashion a simple hook clasp at each end of the wire.

8 Bend the figure's wire "arms" into a V shape. Use pliers to form a hook at the end of each arm. Slip the hooks onto the completed neck wire.

FASHIONING THE TASSEL

9 Cut a 3-inch-long (7.6 cm) piece of the 18-gauge wire. Loop one end of the wire with needle-nose pliers, then wrap the remainder of the tail around the long stem of the wire.

10 Pull seven 1-yard-long (0.9 m) strands of the three-ply waxed linen thread through the wire loop. Knot the strands together in a square knot under the wire loop, with the straight wire pointing upward.

11 Begin with the longest linen thread in the center of the piece. Using a variety of sizes and shapes for interest, string approximately 10 beads on the thread at a time, then tie a square knot. Add another 10 or so beads and tie another knot. Be sure to leave string exposed between the groups of beads to create negative and positive space. When the first linen string is complete, move on to the second longest thread on either side of the finished strand. Repeat this step to bead all of the linen threads.

12 Tie lengths of ribbon or any other flowing materials onto the wire to enhance the beaded strands.

13 Secure a sewing bobbin to the top of the wire form on top of the completed beadwork. Assemble a large collection of found beads or metal objects and attach them to the bobbin by wire-wrapping the items through the bobbin's side holes.

14 Using the remaining wire, thread a bead with a small hole on top of the embellished bobbin, then thread the wire through a hole in one of the keys. Use needle-nose pliers to form a wire loop around the key hole and tighten to secure.

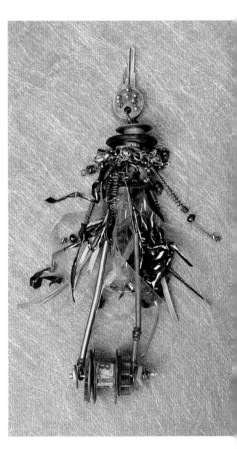

"The Performer is reveling in applause after a deep bow. Found objects help define her body parts. The first altered key, with a long elegant gown attached, is meant to be a singer. The second altered key holds the unicyclist." SUSAN LENART KAZMER

river stone ring

Use this simple and elegant setting to display the natural beauty of an outstanding stone or other found object.

Materials

Sterling silver sheet, 16 gauge

Solder

Bezel wire, 28 gauge, ¼ inch (6 mm) wide

River stone, at least 5/16 inch (8 mm) thick and 5/8 inch (1.6 cm) in diameter

Sterling silver sheet, 20 gauge

Tools & Supplies

Scribe

Straightedge

Jeweler's saw and blades

Flat file

Mallet

Ring mandrel

Soldering kit, see page 35

Bezel mandrel or drill bit

Diamond core drill bit set

Flexible shaft

Diamond twist drill bit set

Center punch

Steel block

Riveting hammer

Small drill bits

Sandpaper, various grits

Polishing compounds (optional)

Two-part epoxy

Step by Step

1 Use the ring sizing chart on page 156 to determine the length of the silver band. Use a scribe and a straightedge to draw the profile of the band onto the 16-gauge silver sheet. (The solder joint for the band will be at the bottom of the ring.)

2 Use the jeweler's saw to cut out the band, leaving a little extra metal outside the scribed lines. Clean up the cut edges with a medium-size flat file.

3 Use the mallet to bend the band around a ring mandrel until its ends meet. File and clean the ends of the bent band to create a good joint for soldering.

4 Flux the joint, solder it with hard solder, then pickle and rinse the band. Use the mallet to reshape the ring on the mandrel, making the band perfectly round.

5 Form the 28-gauge bezel wire around a bezel mandrel to make a small piece of tubing. (The diameter of the tubing should be approximately 2 mm less than the width of the top of the band.) Solder the joint with hard solder. Pickle and rinse the tube.

6 File one end of the tube to match the contour of the top of the band. After making a good fit, solder the tube to the band with medium solder. Pickle and rinse the band.

7 To drill the bottom of the river stone, select a diamond core drill bit that is 2 to 4 mm larger than the diameter of the tube. Slowly drill approximately 3 to 4 mm into the bottom of the stone. The result will be a circular drilled area with a core left inside. To remove the core, drill a series of holes into it with a smaller core drill bit. Repeat this procedure until the entire core is drilled down and a flat-bottomed hole is left.

river stone
ring

NORIKO HANAWA
Florence, 2003
Largest, 1⅜ x 1¼ x ⅝ in. (3.5 x 3.2 x 1.6 cm)
Brick, silver, resin
Photo by Federico Cavicchioli

8 Measure the diameter of the stone's drilled hole and subtract 1 mm from this number. Cut a disk that equals this measurement out of the 20-gauge sterling silver sheet. Check that the metal disk fits inside the drilled hole.

9 Use a diamond twist drill bit (approximately 1.5 mm) to drill a hole in the center of the stone. Drill slowly from the top to the bottom of the stone.

10 Place the silver disk in the bottom of the stone. From the top of the stone, feed a thin scribe or needle through the drilled hole and mark the disk. Use a center punch to dimple the disk on the mark. Using the same size bit used to make the hole in the stone, drill a hole through the disk.

11 Cut a piece of bezel wire the same diameter as the drilled hole. The wire should to be long enough to pass through the stone and extend 3 to 4 mm beyond it. (This wire will be soldered to the disk and become the rivet that holds the stone.) Using hard solder, solder the wire into the hole in the disk. Pickle and rinse the metal. Place the soldered disk and post into the stone to check the fit.

12 Drill a small hole (approximately 1 mm in diameter) through the disk. (This hole allows gases to escape when you solder the disk to the tube on the ring.) Clean the bottom of the disk. Place a generous amount of easy solder on the bottom of the disk and heat to flow. Clean the surface of the tube on the top of the ring. Flux the top of the tube, place the disk on the tube, and solder the seam. Pickle and rinse the ring.

13 Check that the stone fits on the ring. (You can bend the wire slightly in any direction.) The wire should stand above the stone by a little more than half the diameter of the wire.

14 Clean and finish the outside of the ring as desired. (The artist chose a coarse finish and used 180-grit sandpaper on the metal.) Clean and finish three-quarters of the inside of the ring, leaving the remainder as the final step.

15 Tightly clamp the ring mandrel into a bench vise. Following the manufacturer's instructions, mix a small amount of two-part epoxy and place it on the disk and the post. Slide the stone onto the setting. Slide the ring onto the ring mandrel, keeping the underside of the top of the ring flat on the mandrel. (You'll have to hold the ring at an angle to allow for the taper of the mandrel.) Using the riveting hammer, repeatedly strike the center of the wire with concise strokes to flare the rivet head. Hammer from all directions to obtain a nicely domed rivet head.

16 Finish the rivet head as desired or leave the hammered texture. Be sure to remove any sharp burrs. Finish the inside of the ring. (The artist used sandpaper and buffing compounds to achieve a high polish. If a high polish is not desired, use 320-grit sandpaper.)

wire & steel brooch

Combine contrasting materials—rusted steel, electrical wire, and a single cultured pearl—to arrive at an exceptionally dignified sculptural brooch.

wire & steel
brooch

Materials

Rusted steel or other found metal object

Sterling silver wire, square, 2 mm

Sterling silver wire, round, three gauges: 16, 20, and 24 or 26

Solder

Liver of sulfur

Electrical wire

Copper wire, 12 inches (30.5 cm), 24 gauge

Paste wax

Miniature machine screw, washer, and nut, size 1, approximately 72 threads per 1 inch (2.5 cm)

Epoxy

Cultured pearl, half drilled, 4 to 5 mm

Scatter pin clutch

Tools & Supplies

Steel wool

Steel block

Center punch

Chasing hammer

Flexible shaft or small handheld rotary tool

Drill bit, 1.02 mm

Jeweler's saw and saw blades

Sandpaper, 320 grit

Sandpaper, 400 and 600 grit (optional)

Ball-peen or riveting hammer

Flat file

Soldering kit, see page 35

Wire snips

Craft knife

Flat-nose pliers

Small vise (optional)

Step by Step

1 Prepare the surface of the found metal object by removing any loose rust with steel wool and washing it with soapy water.

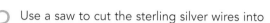

Figure A

2 Mark the locations for the drill holes on the found metal object, using figure A as a template if desired. Dimple each mark, then use a flexible shaft or small handheld rotary tool with a 1.02-mm bit to drill the holes. (These may be enlarged later if necessary.)

3 Use a saw to cut the sterling silver wires into the following lengths:

1 piece of the 2-mm square wire, 1½ inches (3.8 cm) long

1 piece of the 16-gauge round wire, 2½ inches (6.4 cm) long

1 piece of the 20-gauge round wire, 3 inches (7.6 cm) long

1 piece of the 24- or 26-gauge round wire, approximately 2 inches (5 cm) long

4 Sand the metal parts with 320-grit sandpaper. (If a finer finish is desired, continue with 400-grit, then 600-grit paper.)

5 Texture the front side of the piece of square wire with a ball-peen hammer or with the flat end of a riveting hammer. Use a flat file to create an angle on both ends of the wire. Sand the angled wire ends with 320-grit paper.

6 Gently curve the 16-gauge round wire with your fingers, using the project photo on page 123 as a guide. File one end of the curved round wire to fit flush against the top right side of the square wire. Solder this joint with medium solder. Pickle and clean the piece. Oxidize the soldered piece with liver of sulfur, then lighten it to the desired finish with steel wool.

7 Cut the 20-gauge round wire into three 1-inch-long (2.5 cm) sections. File the ends flush. Use these 1-inch (2.5 cm) pieces to make three rivets. (Alternately, you could use miniature bolts for two of these rivets.)

EMANUELA ZAIETTA
Father, 2003
2⅜ x ¹³⁄₁₆ x ¹³⁄₁₆ in. (6 x 2 x 2 cm)
Found iron, 22-karat gold; constructed
Photo by Federico Cavicchioli

CAROLYN BENSINGER
Earrings, 2001
2 x ⅜ x ¼ in. (5.1 x 1 x 0.6 cm)
18-karat rose gold, 14-karat rose gold,
champagne diamonds, found steel; fabricated
Photo by Dean Powell

8 Use snips to cut the electrical wire into two sections. Make one that is approximately 2½ inches (6.4 cm) long and one that is 2¾ inches (7 cm) long. You may wish to cut the wire a bit longer in case you run into a problem stripping the ends or to facilitate your original design. Measure approximately ½ inch (1.3 cm) in from one end of each electrical wire and mark this point. Use a sharp craft knife to gently cut around the rubber coating at the marked point. Strip off the coating to expose the copper wires.

9 On each piece of wire, wrap the section of rubber coating that is adjacent to the exposed copper wires with the 24-gauge copper wire. (These copper wires can be oxidized if desired.) Set aside the partially stripped and wire-wrapped electrical wires.

10 Apply a coat of paste wax to the rusted metal element.

11 File off the threads of the miniature metal machine screw to create a pin stem. Do not file the threads closest to the head of the screw. These are left on to accommodate the thickness of the rusted metal element, the washer, and the nut. Check the fit by inserting the screw into the rusted metal, then attaching the washer and nut. Recheck this periodically as you file. (If you're using a hex-head machine screw, sand down its head as even to the surface of the metal as possible.) Burnish the filed bolt and insert it for the final time, tightly securing it with the washer and nut.

12 Using two of the three rivet wires, rivet the soldered sterling wires to the top of the front of the rusted metal piece.

13 Following the manufacturer's directions, use the epoxy to cleanly adhere the electrical wires to the front of the rusted metal. Insert and epoxy the final rivet wire through the rusted metal to provide a post for the pearl. Let dry.

14 Gently sew the 24- or 26-gauge sterling silver wire in a crisscross direction across the top of the electrical wires. On the back side of the rusted metal object, wrap the loose wire ends around the sewn wires a few times and crimp to secure.

15 Wrap a small piece of the 24- or 26-gauge sterling silver wire around a small dowel a few times to create a looped "seat" for the pearl. Oxidize the looped wire, then place it over the post with the pearl. Check the fit and adjust if necessary. Use epoxy to secure the pearl and let dry. Apply the pin clutch and wear proudly.

TRACK IT DOWN

- Broken or old electronics or appliances are a great source for found wire. The electrical wire in this brooch came out of an old radio.
- Look along sidewalks and in curbs and gullies for small pieces of rusted metal. Passing cars coupled with the effects of the weather beautifully distress the most ordinary of objects.

"Metal in any form and condition always intrigues me, and I couldn't help but pick up this lovely rusted piece while on a walk. I felt the intricacies within the color, texture, and form were quite beautiful. I decided to combine it in a piece of jewelry with electrical wire, another nontraditional material I use often. The juxtaposition of a pearl against rusted metal and black wire provides a startling contrast of elements." MERRY RADTKE

ham bone ring

Bone has been an important material in the history of jewelry. This project is a modern and stylish take on that tradition.

Materials

Ham bone
Sterling silver sheet, 24 gauge
Solder

Tools & Supplies

File
Sandpaper, 220 and 400 grit
Sanding mandrel (optional)
Flexible shaft (optional)
Scribe
Metal ruler
Jeweler's saw and saw blades
Soldering kit, see page 35
Ring mandrel
Rawhide mallet
Large dapping tool
Chasing hammer
Steel wool, fine grit

Step by Step

1 Clean the ham bone by filing and sanding the rough spots to a 400-grit finish. File the inside of the bone to make it more uniform and to fit your ring size. Don't forget that the bone will be lined with silver, so file off a little extra to account for the thickness of the metal. (The 24-gauge silver sheet will add about 1 mm to the inside diameter of the ring.)

2 Measure the height of the ham bone. Add 4 to 5 mm to this measurement. This will be the height of the metal needed for the silver lining.

3 Use the chart on page 156 to determine the length of metal needed for your ring size. Add about 1 mm to this length to account for the thickness of the metal.

4 Use the scribe and a metal ruler to mark a rectangle on the 24-gauge sterling silver sheet that corresponds to the measurements determined in steps 2 and 3. Saw out the silver rectangle. File or sand the cut edges smooth and straight.

5 Bend the sterling silver rectangle so the short sides meet. Adjust the ring as needed to make sure the ends are lined up perfectly. Clean the metal, flux the joint, and solder the seam with hard solder. Pickle the ring and rinse it in water.

6 Use the ring mandrel and the rawhide mallet to form the ring into a perfect circle. File or sand both sides of the ring so the edges are flat and even. Sand the inside of the ring with 220-grit, then 400-grit sandpaper to remove the solder line.

7 Insert the silver ring into the ham bone. Make sure an equal amount of metal extends past each side of the bone. Gently hammer the large dap into the silver lining, tapping once or twice. Turn the ring over and use the dap to tap the other side of the ring. While tapping the metal, make sure equal amounts of silver protrude from each side of the ham bone. Continue tapping the dap into the ring until the metal is flared and the ham bone cannot be removed from the silver lining.

8 Begin gently tapping the metal with the ball side of the chasing hammer. Evenly tap the metal around the ring. Don't try to work on one section of the circle at a time. Turn the ring over and tap on the other side of the lining. Continue tapping the metal until it fits the uneven shape of the ham bone perfectly. Eventually the silver will become a free-form lining that mimics the shape of the ham bone. Sand the silver lining to a 400-grit finish, then rub it with fine-grit steel wool.

"I found the ham bone I had given my dog lying on the living room floor one afternoon. While cleaning the house I put it on my finger. It fit perfectly! I thought, 'I could make a really nice ring out of this ham bone if I lined it with some silver'." JOANNA GOLLBERG

rubber & bead
necklace

Memory wire lets you slip on this terrific reclaimed rubber necklace with ease.

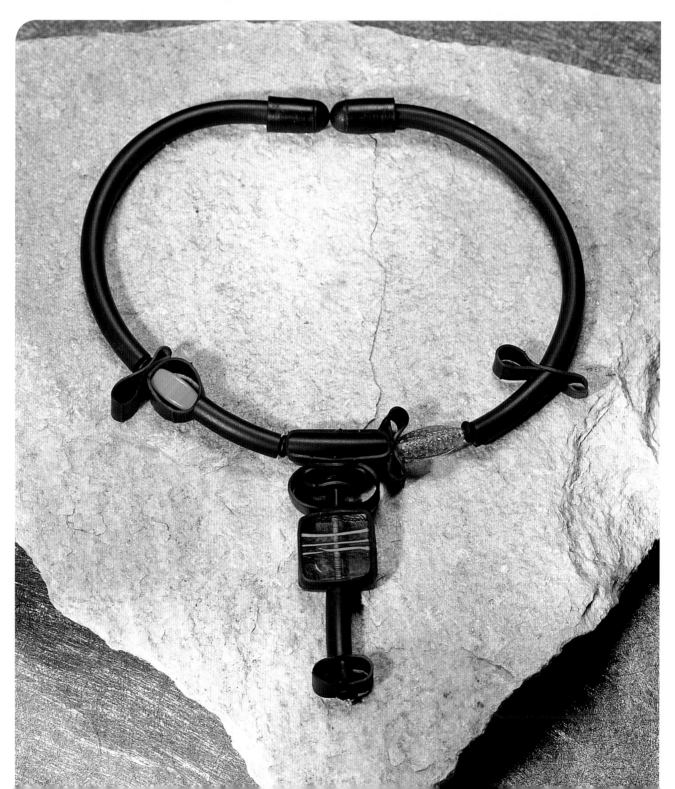

Materials

Bicycle inner tubes, assorted sizes

Vinyl tubing, ¼ inch (6 mm) in diameter*

Stretch cord, clear or black, for beading

Clear fingernail polish

Spacer beads, black (5 small disk beads and 2 large tube beads were used for this necklace)

3 or more glass beads of your choice

Memory wire, example uses 16 inches (40.6 cm)

2 vacuum caps or memory wire end caps

Tools & Supplies

Scissors

Needle with large eye

Wire cutters or snips

File

Flat-nose pliers, 2 pairs

*This type of vinyl tubing is commonly used for landscaping. If you don't have any to recycle, you can purchase it from a hardware store or home improvement center.

Before You Begin

The strength of this project comes from the visual contrast of the black vinyl and rubber against the bright glass beads. Use just a few beads for maximum impact. You can create added interest by creatively looping the rubber, spacing the beads, and leaving areas of plain black rubber and vinyl. To create a bold and successful asymmetrical necklace, it may help you to think in odd numbers as you plan the design.

Step by Step

MAKING THE RUBBER & VINYL BEADS

1 Select one bicycle inner tube. Use sharp scissors to cut across the inner tube, making beads for the necklace that are each ¼ to ⅜ inch (6 to 10 mm) wide. Repeat this step with a variety of sizes of inner tubes. (The featured necklace uses 12 rubber inner tube beads.)

2 Use the sharp scissors to cut various lengths of the vinyl tubing to use as beads. (Four vinyl-tubing beads were used in making this necklace.) For the back of the necklace, cut two additional pieces of the vinyl tubing, each at least 5½ inches (14 cm) long. Incorporate these two tubing pieces as you formulate your necklace design.

MAKING THE PENDANT

3 Cut 12 inches (30.5 cm) of the stretch cord. (This length is excessive, but it makes tying knots much easier.) Depending on the type of cord, make two or three knots on one end. Put a dab of clear fingernail polish on the finished knots if desired.

4 String a small spacer bead on the cord and guide it down to the knotted end. Thread the needle with the loose end of the cord and sew through one side of one inner tube bead. Thread one large spacer bead onto the needle and guide it down the cord. Push the needle through the second side of the inner tube bead.

5 String one vinyl-tubing bead onto the cord. Sew through one side of one inner tube bead, thread a large glass bead on the cord, and push the needle through the second side of the inner tube bead.

6 To create the final, most complex pendant element, sew the beads in this sequence: one side of one large inner tube bead; one large spacer bead; one side of one small inner tube bead; one small spacer bead; the second side of the small inner tube bead; and the second side of the large inner tube bead. Pull snugly—you don't want any slack in the cord.
Tip: You'll probably need to take the needle off the cord every time you add a bead, then put it back on when going through a section of inner tube.

"I make a concerted effort to observe and think creatively. When I look at refuse or parts in the hardware store, I don't think about what it was made to do—I think, 'What I could do with that?'" ELIZABETH A. HAKE

rubber & bead
necklace

ANGELA GLEASON
Complacency (Rosary), 2000
1 x 3 x 12 in. (2.5 x 7.6 x 30.5 cm)
Earplugs, plastic; assembled
Photo by Hap Sakwa

ATTACHING THE PENDANT TO THE WIRE

7 To hide the connection of the pendant to the memory wire, use scissors to cut a piece of vinyl tubing that is approximately 1 inch (2.5 cm) long. Thread the needle with the stretch cord, stick the needle through the center of the 1-inch-long (2.5 cm) vinyl-tubing piece, and pull it out the back side of the vinyl. (If you pulled it out the top of the tube, the knot would be visible.) Pull the cord underneath the back of the tubing, then wrap it around the front side of the cord. Pull the cord snug and knot it several times on the back of the pendant.

8 Use cutters or snips to cut a length of memory wire that is twice the length of the necklace. (For this 16-inch [40.6 cm] necklace, the artist cut a 32-inch [81.3 cm] piece of memory wire.) File the ends of the memory wire smooth.

9 Thread the pendant onto the memory wire. If you made the pendant described above, thread the memory wire through the vinyl tubing at the top of the pendant. Feed the pendant all the way around the circle until it hangs in the center of the memory wire.

BEADING THE REST OF THE NECKLACE

10 String the rest of the beads on the memory wire, building up both sides of the necklace according to your design. Hold the inner tube sections flat between your fingers and push the wire through the rubber. Thread an inner tube bead or two closer to one side of the pendant to create an asymmetrical look. If you want to position a glass bead inside an inner tube bead, push the memory wire through only one side of an inner tube bead, string the glass bead onto the wire, then push the wire through the second side of the inner tube bead. Tip: If you are adding a really long glass bead to the necklace, try slowly rotating the bead while feeding it onto the end of the memory wire. The

vinyl tubing beads easily slide right where you want them. String small spacer beads on the ends of the vinyl tubing beads for a finished look, to hide the hole in the tubing, and to help hold the tubing in place.

11 Add one of the 5½-inch-long (14 cm) pieces of vinyl tubing on one side of the necklace. Once you're pleased with the placement of all elements, pull the memory wire tight on that side. Use two pairs of pliers to bend the leftover wire at a 90-degree angle toward the outside of the necklace. Repeat this process on the other side of the necklace.

12 Cut off the excess memory wire, but leave ⅜ inch (10 mm) of wire sticking out of the vinyl tubing at a right angle. Tip: When cutting memory wire, always point it down toward the floor or hold onto the part you are trimming off. Even if you are wearing safety glasses someone else in the room might not be!

CAPPING THE ENDS

13 Option A (pictured): Using two sets of pliers, bend the excess memory wire over the vinyl tubing. Make two more right angles and push the end of the wire back inside the vinyl tubing. Flatten the wire inside the tubing with pliers. To finish the necklace, place rubber vacuum caps over the ends of the tubing.

Option B: String spacer beads onto the excess memory wire at the ends of the last vinyl tubing pieces. Use an adhesive to attach memory wire end caps.

watch-back choker

Highly detailed and beautifully constructed, watch mechanisms are the focus of this elegant choker.

watch-back choker

"The intricate and delicate detail on the backs of these watches shows the incredible craftsmanship that went into their making and inspired me to use them as the focal points of this necklace. I love highly detailed designs. These watch backs are as beautiful as gemstones." KATHY STOFFEL

Materials

5 to 7 watch mechanisms,
   removed from cases

Glass cleaner

Sterling silver wire, 24 gauge,
   approximately 5 inches (12.7 cm)
   per watch mechanism

Silver jump rings, 22 or 24 gauge,
   3 to 4 mm in diameter

Flexible medium beading wire in silver, clear,
   or bronze, 5 mm

4 silver crimp tubes, 2 x 2 mm

A variety of small beads; for this project,
   the artist used:

   26 silver-lined matte white seed beads, size 110

   80 silver-lined matte white seed beads, size 18

   110 silver seed beads, size 24

   8 silver washers, 6 mm

   4 gold-tone coil beads, 4 mm

Small toggle or lobster claw clasp of your choice

Tools & Supplies

Cotton-tip swabs

Round-nose pliers

Crimping pliers

Before You Begin

Select watches with mechanisms that are mostly intact; these instructions are written for vintage watches with mechanical internal workings (fly wheels), not computer chips. The watches don't have to be in working order.

Step by Step

1 Clean the watch mechanisms carefully, front and back, using a cotton-tip swab dipped in glass cleaner. If the watch faces still have their hour and minute hands, they may catch on clothing. To remove them, snap the hands off with pliers.

WRAPPING & CONNECTING THE WATCH MECHANISMS

2 Cut a 5- to 6-inch (12.7 to 15.2 cm) piece of the silver wire. Create a bend approximately ⅛ inch (3 mm) in from one end of the wire to make a hook. With the back of one watch facing you, place the hook in its bottom opening.

3 Hold the hook in place and bend the wire around the side of the watch. Once the wire reaches the side of the watch, use the following instructions to create a wrapped loop as you would for an earring dangle. Bend the wire at a 90-degree angle to start the loop exactly where you want it. Holding the round-nose pliers approximately ⅛ inch (3 mm) from the bend, wrap the wire around the nose of the pliers to create a loop. Tightly wrap the wire two to three times under the loop. End the wrap with the wire continuing in the same direction around the watch. Push the wrapped loop against the side of the watch, with the loop to the outside. If the wire falls away from the watch at this point, don't worry, just finish the first wrapped loop, place the hook back into the opening at the bottom of the watch, and continue firmly wrapping the wire back around the watch towards the top.

4 If the watch stem is still in place on the mechanism, wrap the wire around the stem once. If the watch no longer has its stem, continue wrapping the wire across the top of the watch.

5 Wrap the wire down the second side of the watch, stopping to create a wrapped loop in approximately the same place you created a loop on the first side. (The loops can be placed in the upper section of the watch or more in the middle of the watch's side, however you prefer.) The loops can be bent gently into position later. (Note: If your watch doesn't have a stem, the wire wrap may not hold onto the watch by itself at this point. Just keep wrapping, maintaining tension, and forming the wire along the outer sides of the watch.)

6 To end the wrap, you have two choices.

• If the mechanism still has its stem, end the wrap by continuing to form the wire up the side of the watch and wrapping it around the stem again. Use the round-nose pliers to gently tighten the wrap around the watch stem.

• If the watch stem is not in place, end the wire wrap at either the bottom opening (where the wrap started) or at any other opening along the outer edge of the watch. To end the wrap along the bottom of the watch, create another hook approximately ⅛ inch (3 mm) in length. Pull the hook into place just inside the opening. Using the needle-nosed pliers, press down firmly on the hook edges to form it against the watch body. Wrap around the entire outer perimeter of the watch one or two times. You can also end the wrap by catching the end of the wire between the watch face and the mechanism.

7 Tighten the wrap anywhere along the outer edges by pushing the wire into an opening and creating a kink in the wire. Doing so increases the tension on the wire and holds it firmly in place. Gently pick up the watch by a loop and make sure its face remains firmly in place within the wire wrap. Use the pliers to gently position the loops so they lay open like ears on either side of the watch.

8 Repeat steps 2 through 7 to wire wrap all of the watches for the choker. (Try to be patient. It may take a little practice and you may have to redo a wrap, but you'll get the hang of it. The key is in using soft wire and the kinking technique to help hold the watch in place.)

9 Lay the watches on your work surface with their back sides facing up and determine the position for each watch in the chocker. Use one jump ring to connect each adjacent pair of wrapped watches by threading the ring through the wire loops. Make sure the watches lay flat and face the same direction.

CREATING THE SIDES OF THE CHOKER

10 Cut two pieces of the beading wire, each approximately 6½ inches (16.5 cm) long, or measure the connected watches and determine the length of wire needed for the sides of the necklace to create the total length you desire. Add a little extra length to the beading wire so you have enough to crimp each end. The total length of the choker pictured is 15½ inches (39.4 cm).

11 Finish one end of the beading wire by creating a loop and securing it with a crimp tube. Following the manufacturer's instructions, use the crimping pliers to create a dimpled crimp tube with the back of the pliers, then curve the crimp tube in on itself using the front part of the crimping pliers.

12 String the beads onto the beading wire in a pleasing combination of seed beads and slightly larger beads. Use any colors or combination of beads you like, or follow the artist's sequence for each side of the necklace. Crimp the end of the beaded wire, then use jump rings to attach one crimped wire end to the clasp and the other to the watch faces.

13 Repeat steps 11 and 12 to create and attach the second beaded side of the choker.

seashell
parure

Create an impressive necklace, bracelet, and earring
suite by collecting and stringing small shells together.

Materials

Round mother-of-pearl beads, 6 to 7 mm, 2 for
 necklace, 2 for bracelet

Silk cord, one package of size 6, color of your choice

Small spiral or cone shells, ½ inch (1.3 cm) long,
 approximately 100

Irregular shell fragments, approximately ¼ inch
 (6 mm), about 35

Medium spiral or cone shells, 1 to 1½ inches
 (2.5 to 3.8 cm) long, approximately 20

Sterling silver wire, 20 gauge, 6 pieces, each
 2½ inches (6.4 cm) long

Sterling bead cones, ¾ inch (1.9 cm), 2 for necklace,
 2 for bracelet

Hypo cement

2 sterling silver jump or split rings, 6 to 7 mm
 in diameter

Sterling silver wire, 16 gauge, 2¼ inches (5.7 cm)
 long, for S hook necklace clasp

Sterling silver toggle clasp, for bracelet

Sterling silver ear wires

Masking tape

Tools & Supplies

Flexible shaft with small drill bit (optional, for drilling
 holes in shells)

Awl or T-pin for hand knotting

Scissors

Chain-nose pliers

Round-nose pliers

Flush wire cutters

Chasing hammer

Before You Begin

All shells and shell fragments must have naturally
occurring or drilled holes. For instructions on how to
drill shells, see page 40. Measurements given are for
an 18½-inch-long (47 cm) necklace and a 7½-inch-
long (19 cm) bracelet.

Step by Step

FOR THE NECKLACE

1 String one of the round 6- to 7-mm mother-of-
pearl beads onto the silk cord. Leave about a
3-inch (7.6 cm) tail at the end of the silk cord for
knotting later. Use a piece of masking tape to hold
the bead in place at this point. Do not shorten the
silk cord. Use the whole strand. (One package of silk
cord will be plenty for stringing the bracelet and the
necklace.) Make an overhand knot and use an awl or
a T-pin to tighten the knot close to the mother-of-
pearl bead. Tip: To make uniform knots that are the
same shape and size, tie each knot by looping the
thread in the same direction each time.

2 String five to six of the small spiral shells. Add
one small shell fragment. Knot the cord below
the fragment to keep the strung shells in place.
Repeat this step until you've created approximately
4½ inches (11.4 cm) of strung shells.

3 Lay out the medium spiral shells and create a
graduated effect with the longest shell in the center of the design and the smallest at both ends. (The
artist used 10 medium spiral shells for this necklace.)

4 String a small shell fragment on the cord. Add
the first (smallest) medium spiral shell. String a
second fragment, then tie an overhand knot.
Tighten the knot. Add two small spiral shells, a fragment, a medium spiral shell, and another fragment.
Tie an overhand knot and tighten. Repeat the
sequence in this step to string all of the medium
spiral shells for the center of the necklace.

"This set was inspired by the fabulous fringed mother-of-pearl jewelry created in the 1930s.
It is a perfect showpiece for those natural gems found along the shore's edge." RACHEL DOW

seashell
parure

5 String a second length of the small spiral shells and the shell fragments to match the completed side. String a mother-of-pearl bead to finish the strand. Measure about 3 inches (7.6 cm) beyond the last bead and cut the silk cord at this point. Place a piece of masking tape close to the last bead to keep the strung shells in place. Set the leftover silk cord aside.

6 Using the chain-nose pliers, make a right angle close to the center of one end of one 2½-inch (6.4 cm) piece of the 20-gauge sterling silver wire. Use the round-nose pliers to lightly grasp the wire at the right angle. With your other hand, wrap the wire around the top of the pliers to make a loop. Use the chain-nose pliers to lightly grasp the loop on the opposite side. Use your other hand to wrap the wire around the neck of the loop two to three times. When wrapping the wire, pull tight. Cut off the excess wire with the flush cutters.

7 Test the wire loop size by placing the bead cone over it. The bead cone should easily cover the wire loop without it showing. (If you need to adjust the loop size, use the chain-nose pliers and gently squeeze the loop together into more of an oval shape. Retest the shape by placing the bead cone over the loop.)

8 To string the wire loop onto the necklace ends, thread one tail end of the silk cord through the wire loop and tie an overhand knot. Use the wire

loop to tighten the knot close to the round mother-of-pearl bead on the end of the necklace. Tie two or three more overhand knots through the wire loop to make a secure attachment. Place a dab of hypo cement on the knots and let dry. Repeat steps 6, 7, and 8 to knot the other end of the necklace.

9 Cut off the tail ends of the silk cord. Slip one bead cone onto the wire. Follow the process in step 6 to make another wire-wrapped loop to secure the bead cone in place. Before wire wrapping the wire end, slip a jump or split ring onto the loop. Repeat this step on the opposite end of the necklace.

10 Use the 2¼-inch (5.7 cm) piece of 16-gauge wire to make the S hook clasp. Hammer both ends of the wire, approximately ¼ inch (6 mm) in from each end. Use the round-nose pliers to make a small circle on each hammered wire end. Form the ends so the circles bend in opposite directions. About halfway up the length of the wire, bend it with the round-nose pliers to make a loop. Bend the wire away from your body so the small circle on the end faces the opposite direction. Turn the clasp around and make another loop, bending it away from your body again and reversing the direction of the loop. The clasp should now have an S shape. Using the chasing hammer, hammer the curves of the clasp slightly to harden them. Adjust the gaps in the wire as needed. One jump ring stays firmly secured in the clasp while the other is able to snap or slide into place and secure the necklace.

NICOLE JACQUARD
Australia-Shadow Box Pin, 1999
2 x 1 x ½ in. (5.1 x 2.5 x 1.3 cm)
22-karat gold, 18-karat gold, shells,
pearls, sea urchin quills, glass
Photo by Kevin Montague

PIERRE CAVALAN
Inner Peace Committee, 2002
4¾ x 3½ x ⅝ in. (12 x 8.9 x 1.6 cm)
Mixed media, aluminum, enamel,
badges; anodized
Photo by Terry Constanti

FOR THE BRACELET

1 Follow step 1 for creating the shell necklace, then string an alternating pattern of small spiral shells, medium spiral shells, and shell fragments down the full length of the cord. As you string the shells on the cord, measure the bracelet to make sure it is the right length. Remember to include the bead cones and toggle clasp in your measurement.

2 Once you've strung the correct length of shells, finish off both ends of the bracelet as described in steps 6 through 9 of the necklace instructions. Instead of attaching jump rings, however, attach the toggle clasp. Adjust the wire loops so the toggle clasp ends move freely.

FOR THE EARRINGS

1 Cut two pieces of 20-gauge wire, each 2½ inches (6.4 cm) long. Make a loop on one end of each wire piece, as described in step 6 of the necklace instructions.

2 String one small shell fragment and two small spiral shells on the wire. Before wrapping the opposite end of the wire, slip a medium spiral shell on the loop. Wrap the loose wire end around the neck of the wire. Repeat this step on the second wire. Attach the shell dangles to the sterling silver ear wires.

Variations

• Change the length of the necklace.
• Mix spiral shells with shells of other shapes.
• Add more shell dangles to the earrings.
• Make a multistranded necklace or bracelet.

CHECK IT OUT

Between 50,000 and 200,000 mollusk species live today. Horns, Augers, and Ceriths are common varieties with long spiral shells. Most species have shell whorls that coil in a clockwise direction. If you find one of these shells in the water rather than washed up on shore, chances are it still has a resident creature.

driftwood
brooch

Enhance the beauty of driftwood with a few wisely chosen found elements to create an attractive synthesis of nature and industry.

"I found this wonderful piece of driftwood on the shores of Lake Erie. The water provided it with an amazing sheen that I couldn't resist. I knew it would find its way into a unique body ornament, and when it did I returned to the same beach to pick up the perfect pebble as its companion." MERRY RADTKE

Materials

Driftwood

Beach pebble

Copper plumbing tubing, ¼-inch (6 mm) outside
   diameter

Sterling silver wire, square, 1 mm

Sterling silver round wire, 20 or 18 gauge

Solder

Liver of sulfur

Epoxy

Rubber wire grommet, ½-inch (1.3 cm) outside
   diameter, ¼-inch (6 mm) inside diameter

2 brass-center snap-on sanding disks, centers only

Paste wax

Scatter pin clutch

Tools & Supplies

Sandpaper, 320 grit

Sandpaper, 400 and 600 grit (optional)

Calipers

Setting burr (optional)

Flexible shaft or small handheld rotary tool

Jeweler's saw and saw blades

Flat file

Soldering kit, see page 35

Drill bit, 0.94 mm

Needle file, square

Steel wool

Flat prong pusher

Burnisher

Round-nose pliers

Flat-nose pliers

Step by Step

1 If you live near water, take a walk along the
beach or shore and look for an interesting piece
of driftwood. If water isn't nearby, visit the woods for
dry, dead wood. (The artist used a Y-shaped piece,
which should be easy to find.) Then look for a variety of small pebbles that you can sort through later
for setting into the copper tube. Tip: Bring a section
of the copper tube with you to determine the correct pebble size.

2 Sand the sterling silver wires and the copper
tubing with 320-grit sandpaper. (If desired, you
can sand the metals to a finer finish by continuing
with a 400-grit, then a 600-grit paper.)

3 Select a beach pebble to use in the brooch. If
the stone is flat on at least one side, measure
across its width with the calipers and select a setting
burr to match this dimension. If the stone is more
free-form and fits into the copper tube without slipping down into it, proceed to step 5.

4 Use the jeweler's saw to cut a section of copper
tubing approximately 3 inches (7.6 cm) long.
Burr a seat for the pebble in the end of the tube.
(Having a longer section of tubing is easier to handle than a small section. You'll later cut the tube to
the correct dimension.)

5 Measure and cut the metal parts to the dimensions that fit your driftwood and pebble. Since
you can always saw off excess metal, you might
want to make the pieces a bit longer than you think
you need. For this piece, the dimensions were as
follows: a 2½-inch (6.4 cm) piece of square sterling
silver wire, a 1-inch (2.5 cm) piece of round wire, and
a ½ inch (1.3 cm) piece of copper tubing.

driftwood
brooch

6 Determine where the square sterling silver wire should bend to a 90-degree angle, and mark this place on the wire. (This is an aesthetic decision. On this piece, the wire was scored and bent 1 inch [2.5 cm] from one end.) Score and bend the wire to make a clean, crisp angle. If you have trouble with the wire moving while scoring the angle, use masking tape to secure the wire ends to your work surface.

7 Solder the scored and bent wire with hard solder to reinforce the joint. (Without soldering, the joint will be unstable and the wire will break into two parts.)

8 Check the angled square wire against the driftwood to make sure its dimension is correct. Determine where the wire ends will fit into the driftwood, moving it around to see where it looks best, and mark these two locations.

9 Select a drill bit that is slightly smaller than the 1-mm square wire. Drill into one marked point on one side of the driftwood. Recheck the wire with the driftwood to make sure it still lines up with the second mark for the next hole. If the other end of the wire lines up, drill the second hole. If not, adjust the mark, then drill. Use the square needle file to open up the drilled holes, creating square holes to match the wire. Insert the ends of the wire into the holes in the driftwood to check the fit.

10 Use medium solder to solder the copper tubing onto the long section of the sterling square wire, approximately ½ inch (1.3 cm) from the

90-degree angle. Turn over the square wire and use easy solder to solder the ½-inch (1.3 cm) piece of round wire (the pin stem) behind the tubing. This wire piece faces the body when the brooch is worn. Pickle and clean the soldered metal.

Tip: When soldering the round wire, drill a little hole into the firebrick that matches the diameter of the tube. Place the tube into the hole, insert straight pins on either side of the square wire, then solder. Doing so helps hold things in place and prevents the tube from shifting or falling off.

11 Oxidize the metal with the liver of sulfur. Using steel wool, lightly rub the patina to lighten it to the desired finish.

12 Place the pebble in the tube. Using a flat prong pusher, push the metal rim on the outside of the tube onto the stone. (If the pebble shifts, use a tiny bit of epoxy to hold it in place.) Use a burnisher to smooth out the rim and to make it glimmer. Place the rubber grommet over the tubing and stone.

13 Using the round-nose and flat-nose pliers, gently bend the sanding disk inserts. Ever so slightly, bend and fit them against the curve of the driftwood and around the square holes that will hold the soldered metal part.

14 Polish the driftwood with paste wax if desired. (The artist's driftwood had a beautiful sheen, so she used the paste wax to protect this natural finish.)

CLAUDIA RINNEBERG
Solutions, 2003
Iron, fine gold
Photo by Frederico Cavicchioli

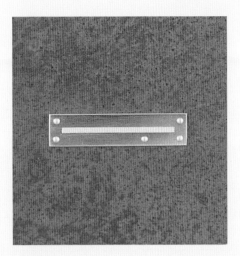

ABRASHA
Square Pin #8, 1990
2 x 2 x ¹³⁄₁₆ in. (5.1 x 5.1 x 2 cm)
Rusted steel, 18-karat gold, 24-karat
gold, sterling silver, stainless steel;
fabricated, cold connected
Photo by artist

15 Snip off the round wire (pin stem) to a dimension that works with the pin clutch. File the end of the wire to a point and soften it with sandpaper. Using flat-nose pliers, grab this wire lengthwise and twist it to work harden the metal. Burnish the stem to smooth and finish it.

16 Join all the brooch parts together to recheck their fit. Use epoxy to glue the sanding disk inserts onto the driftwood and the square wire into the square holes. Let dry and enjoy!

CHECK IT OUT

Driftwood is a gnarled memory, the testimony of a fallen tree, a downed ship, or perhaps even an abandoned bat or paddle. As the shorelines of beaches and lakes shift with each passing day, so too do the weathered faces of driftwood. Consider yourself lucky to capture this symbol of survival. The hunt is as exciting as finding the perfect piece with which to work.

TRACK IT DOWN

• Brass-center snap on sanding disks have a central brass piece with a square hole that snaps onto a flexible shaft mandrel. Sometimes this part separates from a worn sanding disk when the disk is replaced. When this happens, save this brass centers to reuse in new ways.

• The artist used copper tubing she found in her garage. If you don't have any scraps on hand, copper tubing is sold at building supply companies and hobby stores.

• Rubber grommets are available at auto parts stores The hole at the center of these grommets is used for holding electrical wires.

rose petal **necklace**

Preserve your garden long past the growing season by making a pressed petal necklace.

Materials

Roses

Laminating film, 5 to 7 mm

Bar-link chain, length of your choice, handmade (see page 145) or purchased

Sterling silver round wire, 22 gauge for large jump rings, 24 gauge for small jump rings, and other assorted gauges depending on project style

Solder

Sterling silver sheet, 24 gauge, or sterling chain ends

Sterling silver tubing, thin wall, 1- to 2-mm outside diameter

Tools & Supplies

Flower press or heavy books

Blotter paper or untextured paper towels

Laminating machine (available at photocopy shops)

Scissors

Mandrel for large jump rings

Jeweler's saw and saw blades

Pliers, preferably with parallel jaw

Soldering kit, see page 35

Mandrel, 1 mm in diameter, for small jump rings

Tube-cutting jig (optional)

Fine file

Small drill bits

Anvil or steel block

Center punch

Chasing hammer

Flexible shaft

Small dapping punch

Small hole punch (for paper)

Awl, tapered scribe, or other pointed tool

Riveting hammer

Abrasive wheels or sandpaper

Abrasive scrub pad

Step by Step

MAKING THE LAMINATED ROSE PETALS

1 Determine what form you would like the finished necklace to take. Would you like a full necklace, with rose petals encircling the wearer's neck, or a lariat style, with a more central focal point? Select the roses to use for the necklace. Choose roses for pressing that are as freshly cut as possible.

2 Decide how many petals you're likely to use in the final necklace and press extra so you can adjust this number as the necklace evolves. Remove the individual petals from the flowers (saying, "he loves me, he loves me not" is optional) and place them between pieces of blotter paper in a flower press. If you don't have access to a press, placing your petals between pieces of unpatterned paper towels under a stack of heavy books works fine. Let the petals press for at least two weeks.

3 Pressed petals are quite fragile. In order to make them durable enough to wear, they must be laminated in acetate. Handling the pressed petals carefully, place them between sheets of laminating film. Be sure to leave about ½ inch (1.3 cm) of space between the petals for trimming later. Send the film through the thermal laminator. Let cool.

4 Trim around the petals, leaving about ⅛ inch (3 mm) of acetate around the perimeter to prevent delamination. Based on color, shape, size, and overall balance, choose the petals to use for the project and set them aside.

Constructing the Necklace Framework

5 If you're making a full petal necklace, first construct the chain. (A bar-link chain is recommended.) Once you have the chain length required for your necklace, add large, 22-gauge jump rings to each existing jump ring between the bars. The diameter of the jump ring will depend on how many petals you attach to each link. Solder the jump rings closed.

rose petal necklace

If you're making a lariat, you need to build a structure to keep the petals from bunching up. In this example, the artist created a central spine of flattened sterling silver wire (at least 18 gauge), to which she soldered one jump ring for every rose petal attached. This method ensures that each petal moves independently, preventing them from stacking up at the end of the chain. You can add crosspieces to the spine if you need more room to solder the jump rings, or you can experiment with bending the spine into a different shape.

MAKING A STURDY ATTACHMENT FOR EACH PETAL

6 If you simply punched holes in the laminated petals and attached them to the necklace with jump rings, they would eventually tear off. Instead, tube rivet each petal to a loop of sterling silver sheet. The silver loop won't tear, and the jump ring can be threaded through it. If you only have a few petals to rivet, you can saw the loop shape out of 24-gauge sterling silver sheet (see figure A). If you have many petals to rivet, commercial silver chain ends will work very well. Choose those with a flange that's at least 1 mm wider than the rivet tube's diameter. Use pliers to bend the chain ends around a nail until its sides are parallel (see figure B).

Figure A

Figure B

7 Anneal 12-inch (30.5 cm) lengths of sterling silver tubing. Cut the tubing to rivet length. Each piece should be only about 2 to 3 mm long. The more consistently you cut the tubing (keeping each piece the same length and keeping the ends perpendicular), the better the rivets will be. (The artist finds it useful to use a tube-cutting jig with a very fine [8/0 or smaller] saw blade. Use a fine file to remove any burrs from the cut tubes.

8 Select a drill bit that corresponds exactly with the outside diameter of the tubing. Use a center punch to dimple the flanges of the flattened loops, then drill the holes on a wood surface.

9 Use the small punch to make a hole near the edge of each laminated petal, where the silver loop will be attached. Slide the punched petal between the flanges of the silver loop and line up the holes. Leave no gaps between petal and silver. Slide a piece of the cut tubing through the holes, leaving the same amount sticking out on each side.

10 Use an awl, tapered scribe, or other pointed tool to begin gently flaring out both sides of the tube. Once both sides are flared equally and the tube no longer slides in and out of the hole, hold the petal slightly above the bench block (use a cardboard spacer if it helps) and dap the top end of the tube to open it further. Flip the piece and repeat on the other side. When both sides are opened by the dapping punch, use the riveting hammer to finish the tube rivet. Remove any hammer marks with abrasive wheels or sandpaper, and finish the riveted silver loop with an abrasive pad.

ATTACHING THE PETALS TO THE CHAIN

11 Finish the necklace by attaching the rose petals to the chain with 24-gauge silver jump rings. Make sure to tightly close the jump rings.

Note: Like most things in nature, the color of laminated rose petals changes with time. In general, colors darken. Yellows may become more umber, and reds deepen to almost black velvet. Keeping your laminated petals out of direct sunlight will help slow this process if you find it undesirable.

"I consistently find myself drawn to the found object, with all its history and inherent character. Often incorporating text or images, I try to transcend the object's preconceived role by stripping it down to its most basic elements and framing it with careful craftsmanship and clean design. Whether including actual text or found objects, or only subtle references to these sources of inspiration, I hope my work offers the viewer and wearer an inside peek at the intrinsic value of the often overlooked." KRISTIN MITSU SHIGA

Constructing a Bar-Link Chain

Materials

Sterling silver wire, at least 18 gauge, for bars
Sterling silver jump rings, 24 gauge, approximately
   3-mm outside diameter
Solder
Handmade or commercial clasp

Tools & Supplies

Mallet or vise (optional)
Flush-cut nippers
Anvil or steel block
Flat-faced chasing tool
Chasing hammer
Center punch
Small drill bits
Flexible shaft
Files or sandpaper
Chain-nose pliers, 2 pairs
Soldering kit, see page 35
Abrasive scrubbing pad

Step by Step

1 Choose a length for the bar sections of the chain. (The artist recommends making bar sections that are each approximately 1 to 2 cm, depending on whether she plans to curve the links or not.) You can also make graduated links if you desire.

2 Straighten the 18-gauge wire by hand, with a mallet, or by pulling it in a vise. (To make a curved bar-link necklace, start with an even curve in the wire.) Cut the straightened wire into 1- to 2-cm

lengths. The finished length of the chain will determine the total number of links you need. It's always a good idea to make a few extra wire lengths.

3 Line up the 18-gauge wire lengths on the anvil or steel block. (To keep the wires from bouncing around, you may want to place masking tape on the steel block with the sticky side up, then put the wires on the tape with both ends sticking off. Remove any tape residue after doing this.) Use the flat-faced chasing tool and chasing hammer to flatten the last 2 mm of each end of each link.

4 Use a center punch to dimple the flattened ends of each link. Drill each dimple with a bit that is large enough for the jump rings to pass through without binding. Make sure to leave as much metal between the hole and the edge of the link as possible. File and sand any rough edges on the links, and make them as uniform as possible. Remove burrs from the drilled holes if necessary.

5 Attach each link with a jump ring, making sure it moves freely. Once the necklace is the correct length, solder the jump rings closed. Attach a handmade or purchased clasp, and use an abrasive pad to give the chain a matte finish if desired.

TRACK IT DOWN

• Consider using roses from a special event to create commemorative jewelry. The artist has made several necklaces for people using roses from weddings and birthdays.

wrap-around rubber bracelet

All you need is a pair of scissors and some ingenuity to fashion a recycled inner tube into an ultramodern accessory.

Materials

Recycled bicycle inner tube, large diameter
Bead, optional (for variation, page 149)
Needle, optional (for variation, page 149)
Waxed thread, optional (for variation, page 149)

Tools & Supplies

Scissors
Roller-ball pen
Needle-nose pliers

Step by Step

1 Cut a 21-inch-long (53.3 cm) section of the bicycle inner tube. Make sure the section you select has no holes, rips, patches, or valve stem.

2 Flatten the inner tube section on a table and measure its width (inner tube sizes vary greatly). Calculate two-thirds of this width.

3 Hold the inner tube section close to one end and flatten it between your fingers. Use the scissors to cut slits two-thirds of the way across the width of the inner tube through both sides of the tube at once. Cut each slit ¼ inch (6 mm) apart for 7 inches (17.8 cm). Cut each slit the same length, parallel to the last.

4 Lay the inner tube over your wrist with decorative slits facing up. Wrap the tube around your wrist. Does the cut area overlap by about 1 inch (2.5 cm)? If the overlap is smaller, cut more slits in the tube until it overlaps 1 inch (2.5 cm). If the overlap of the slit tube is more than or equal to 1 inch (2.5 cm), proceed to the next step.

5 Use the roller-ball pen to draw a small line at the top of the last decorative slit toward the solid end of the tubing (see figure A, line 1). Make a second mark on the bottom side of the last slit (see figure A, line 2).

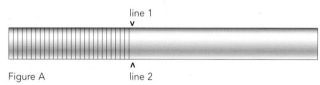

line 1
Figure A   line 2

6 Measure the distance between the two marks, and make corresponding marks down the length of the solid tubing (see figure B). Cut lengthwise down the sides of the tubing, following the marks in figure B. Cut one marked side at a time, using the seams on the inner tube as visual guidelines to help you cut straight. The cut rubber (know hereafter as the strap end) should look like the piece illustrated in figure C.

Figure B

Figure C

7 Cut the end of the rubber strap to the shape shown in figure D. This will be the tab mechanism used to hold the bracelet together.

Figure D

wrap-around rubber bracelet

8 Place the strap end into the opposite slitted end of the inner tube. Carefully feed the strap all the way through the tube until the first and last decorative slits are touching. Make sure the slitted rubber strips remain straight.

9 Place the rubber bracelet on your wrist and see if it fits. If more than two decorative slits overlap, cut them off the end that still resembles a tube (opposite the strap end).

10 With the bracelet still on your wrist, hold the strap end under the slits and use a roller-ball pen to mark where the first notch lays on the inside of the bracelet. Don't make the bracelet too tight. When finished, it will stretch to get over your hand and will fit loosely on your wrist.

11 Loosen the strap from the bracelet and take it apart. Mark the point where the first notch in the strap laid on top of the solid piece of the strap.

12 Measure the width of the strap and mark the center. Fold the strap in half lengthways and cut ⅜ inch (10 mm) up from the fold on the mark made in step 9 (see figure E, line 1).

Figure E

13 Cut a second, identical slit that is ½ inch (1.3 cm) closer to the end of the strap (see figure E, line 2). Cut a third identical slit ½ inch

(1.3 cm) closer to the end of the strap (see figure E, line 3). Three cuts are now perpendicular to the strap edges and ½ inch (1.3 cm) apart.

14 Place the strap in the tube and feed it all the way through to the connection area. Following figure F, insert the strap's arrow tip into the first connector slit, then push it back up through the second slit. Pull the strap until the first notch catches on the first slit. Use a pair of needle-nose pliers to insert the arrow end into the third and final slit. Make sure the strap end lays flat. If any of the slitted rubber pieces overlap you can remove them, but usually the bracelet gives a bit and there is no overlap.

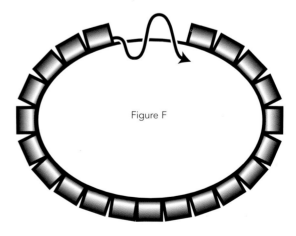

Figure F

EMIKO OYE
Pioneer a Movement, from the *Patent Pending Collection*, 1999
4 in. (10.2 cm) in diameter
Recycled plastic price tags, recycled plastic film, recycled rubber, sterling silver, steel
Photo by artist

Variation

To make this bracelet, weave the strap under one slitted rubber piece and over the next, repeating this sequence all the way around the form. Because some of the strap length is used in weaving the slits, fully weave the bracelet before marking the placement of the connection slits.

If you want to add a bead, determine and mark its location while wearing the bracelet. Use a needle to sew through the rubber and waxed linen thread to string the bead. Sew the bead onto the rubber while the bracelet is taken apart. Tie a double knot in the waxed thread and sew from the back of the strap so the knots are hidden when the bracelet is complete.

CHECK IT OUT

Inner tube rubber is a relatively easy material to transform by hand. You can manipulate it in a similar manner to leather, and in fact, rubber has replaced leather in many applications. The tools required for making rubber jewelry are not expensive and are few in number. Recycling rubber tubes into wearable art is not only a progressive and eco-friendly activity that results in less waste and less environmental degradation, it also produces accessories that are sturdy, waterproof, and completely original.

TRACK IT DOWN

- Many auto garages pay waste disposal companies to remove old inner tubes. (Up to 70 percent of which are later burned or buried in landfills.) Drop by your local auto body shop or bike store and ask them to donate a few old tubes to your creative cause.
- Look for inner tubes on the side of roads and highways. In a single stop, you can make a fabulous find and help control litter.
- Not all inner tubes are made from black rubber. Other colors are available, but more difficult to find. Patient and persistent searching will eventually pay off.

KRISTI ZEVENBERGEN
Spice Cabinet, 2004
2¼ x 16 x ¼ in. (5.7 x 40.6 x 0.6 cm)
Fine silver, sterling silver, recycled perfume sample vials,
spices, tin, copper alloy; knitted, fabricated
Photos by Doug Yaple

J. FRED WOELL
Fishing for Democracy, 2003
2½ x 6¼ x ¾ in. (6.4 x 15.9 x 1.9 cm)
Aluminum, brass, copper, paper, steel, plastic
Photo by artist

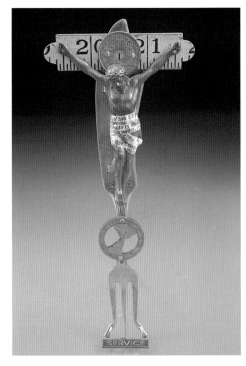

NISA BLACKMON
Revelations: Eat, 2001
6 x 3 x ½ in. (15.2 x 7.6 x 1.3 cm)
Sterling silver, found objects,
acrylic paint; riveted
Photo by artist

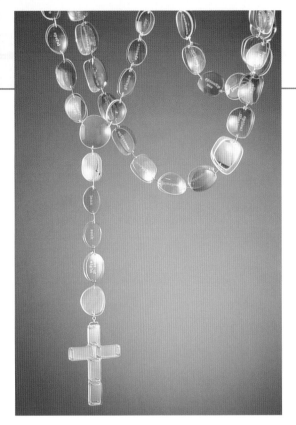

ANGELA GLEASON
Failure to Communicate (Rosary), 2001
2 x ½ x 7 in. (5.1 x 1.3 x 17.8 cm)
Prescription lenses, silver, vinyl letters, mirror, dye
Photo by Hap Sakwa

LINDA KAYE-MOSES
Masqued I, 2002
4½ x 1½ x ½ in. (11.4 x 3.8 x 1.3 cm)
Sterling silver, fine silver, 14-karat gold,
vitreous enamel, variscite, found coin,
metal clay; roller-printed, soldered
Photo by Evan Soldinger

HARRIETE ESTEL BERMAN
Prestige, Value, and Identity, 2001
Largest, 6¼ in. (15.9 cm) in diameter
Preprinted steel from recycled tin
containers, brass, plastic core
Photo by Philip Cohen

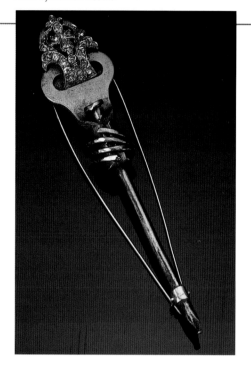

BRAD WINTER
Peep Show No. 1—Coin-Operated Locket, 2000
2¾ x 2 ¾ x ¾ in. (7 x 7 x 1.9 cm)
Sheet metal, steel, springs, wood, found image,
dimes not included; fabricated
Photo by Tom Mills

J. FRED WOELL
Summer Memories/Campabello, 1991
3 x 3 x ¾ in. (7.6 x 7.6 x 1.9 cm)
Copper, stone, brass, silver
Photo by artist

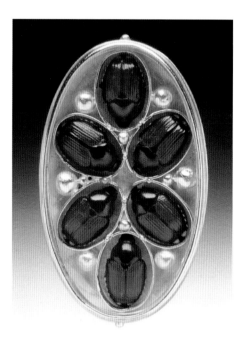

JENNIFER TRASK
Popillia Japonica, 2001
1½ x ¹⁵⁄₁₆ x ⅜ in. (3.8 x 2.4 x 1 cm)
18-karat gold, 22-karat gold,
Japanese beetles, mineral crystal
Photo by Dean Powell
Collection of Kenneth Trapp

KEN THIBADO
Concern, 2002
1⅜ x 1⁵⁄₁₆ x 1/4 in. (3.5 x 3.3 x 0.6 cm)
Found objects, 14-karat gold, sterling silver,
synthetic stones, resin
Photo by Robert Diamante

ELIZABETH A. HAKE
Drape, 2002
12 x 21 x 2 in. (30.5 x 53.3 x 5.1 cm)
Inner tube from truck tire, aluminum
tubing, leather washers; hand cut, riveted
Photo by David A. Hake

J. FRED WOELL
There's No Place Like Home, 1995
4¾ x 4½ x ⁵⁄₁₆ in. (12 x 11.4 x 0.8 cm)
Brass, copper, silver
Photo by artist

KIMBERLY NAVRATIL-POPE
Nonpareil Neckpiece, 2003
18 in. (45.7 cm) long
Sterling silver, nonpareil candies, sugar,
packaging paper; cast, fabricated
Photo by Dean Adams

CANDIE COOPER
Home, 2003
6 x 1½ x ½ in. (15.2 x 3.8 x 1.3 cm)
Enamel, copper, silver, thermoplastic,
paper, domino; fabricated
Photo by Robin Kraft

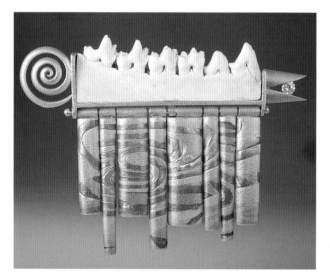

AARON MACSAI
Jawbone Pin, 2001
2¼ x 1½ in. (5.7 x 3.8 cm)
Found jawbone, 18-karat gold, 14-karat
yellow gold; fabricated, polished
Photo by artist

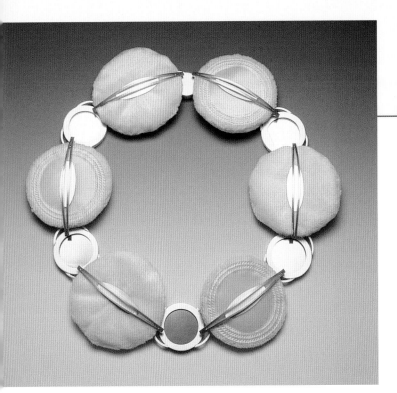

TARA STEPHENSON
Select Cover Up, 2001
½ x 8 x 8 in. (1.3 x 20.3 x 20.3 cm)
Velvet powder puffs, sterling silver, mirrors;
soldered, tab and slot, screwed, sewn
Photos by Dennis Nahabetian

EMIKO OYE
Truth 1: Infotainment, 2002
21 in. (53.3 cm) long
Recycled thermoplastic sheet, recycled plastic film,
fine silver, sterling silver; cold constructed
Photo by Hap Sakwa

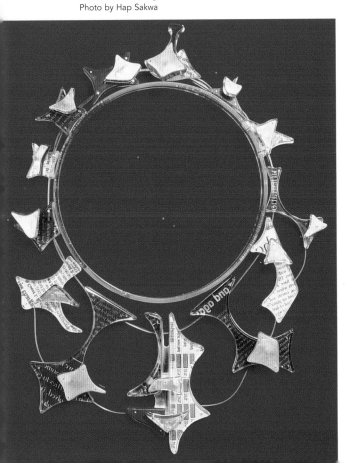

PIERRE CAVALAN
Life Is a Myriad of Experience, 1996
7⅞ x 7⅞ x ⅝ in. (20 x 20 x 1.6 cm)
Mixed media, aluminum, enamel, badges; anodized
Photo by Julian Wolkenstein

charts

THE BROWN AND SHARP (B. & S.) GAUGE FOR SHEET METAL

Gauge Number	Thickness in inches	Thickness in millimeters
3/0	.409	10.388
2/0	.364	9.24
1/0	.324	8.23
1	.289	7.338
2	.257	6.527
3	.229	5.808
4	.204	5.18
5	.181	4.59
6	.162	4.11
7	.144	3.66
8	.128	3.24
9	.114	2.89
10	.101	2.565
11	.090	2.28
12	.080	2.03
13	.071	1.79
14	.064	1.625
15	.057	1.447
16	.050	1.27
17	.045	1.114
18	.040	1.016
19	.035	.889
20	.031	.787
21	.028	.711
22	.025	.635
23	.022	.558
24	.020	.508
25	.017	.431
26	.015	.381
27	.014	.376
28	.012	.304
29	.011	.29
30	.01	.254
31	.008	.203
32	.0079	.199
33	.007	.177
34	.006	.152
35	.0055	.142
36	.005	.127

RING SIZING

USA Size	Diameter in inches	Diameter in mm	Circumference in mm	British Size	French Size	German Size	Japanese Size	Swiss Size
2	.520	13.21	41.5	D	41½	13½	2	1½
2¼		13.41	42.1	D ½				
2½	.536	13.61	42.7	E	42¾	13¾	3	2¾
2¾		13.83	43.4	E ½				
3	.553	14.05	44.0	F	44	14	4	4
3⅛		14.15	44.3	F ½				
3¼		14.25	44.6					
3⅜		14.36	44.9	G	45¼		5	5¼
3½	.569	14.45	45.2			14½		
3⅝		14.56	45.6	G ½			6	
3¾		14.65	45.9	H	46½			6½
4	.585	14.86	46.5	H ½		15	7	
4¼		15.04	47.1	I	47¾			7¾
4½	.601	15.27	47.8	I ½		15¼	8	
4⅝		15.40	48.1	J	49	15½		9
4¾		15.53	48.4					
5	.618	15.70	49.0	J ½		15¾	9	
5⅛		15.80	49.3	K	50			10
5¼		15.90	49.6					
5⅜		16.0	50.0	K ½			10	
5½	.634	16.10	50.3	L	51¾	16		11¾
5¾		16.30	50.9					
5⅞		16.41	51.3	L ½				
6	.650	16.51	51.5	M	52¾	16½	12	12¾
6¼		16.71	52.2	M ½				
6½	.666	16.92	52.8	N	54	17	13	14
6¾		17.13	53.4	N ½				
7	.683	17.35	54.0	O	55¼	17¼	14	15¼
7¼		17.45	54.7	O ½				
7½	.699	17.75	55.3	P	56½	17¾	15	16½
7¾		17.97	55.9	P ½				
8	.716	18.19	56.6	Q	57¾	18	16	17¾
8¼		18.35	57.2	Q ½				
8½	.732	18.53	57.8			18½	17	
8⅝		18.61	58.4	R	59			19
8¾		18.69	58.4					
8⅞		18.80	59.0	R ½				
9	.748	18.89	59.1			19	18	
9⅛		19.10	59.4	S	60¼			20¼
9¼		19.22	59.7					
9⅜		19.31	60.0	S ½				
9½	.764	19.41	60.3			19½	19	
9⅝		19.51	60.6	T	61½			21½
9¾		19.62	60.9					
10	.781	19.84	61.6	T ½		20	20	
10¼		20.02	62.2	U	62¾		21	22¾
10½	.797	20.20	62.8	U ½		20¼	22	
10⅝		20.32	63.1	V	63			23¾
10¾		20.44	63.5					
11	.814	20.68	64.1	V ½		20¾	23	

contributing artists

ANNEALING TEMPERATURES FOR METAL

Metal	Fahrenheit	Celsius
Copper	700°–1200°	370°–650°
Brass	800°–1380°	430°–750°
Silver	1120°–1300°	600°–700°
Gold (other than fine gold)	1200°–1380°	650°–750°

MELTING TEMPERATURES FOR METAL

Metal	Fahrenheit	Celsius
Aluminum	1220°	660°
Gold (other than fine gold)	1600°–1830°	880°–1000°
Silver	1640°	890°
Brass	1660°	900°
Bronze	1945°	1060°
Copper	1980°	1080°
Nickel silver	2020°	1110°
Stainless steel	2500°	1371°
Low carbon steel	2750°	1511°
Iron	2793°	1535°

SOLDER FLOW POINTS

Solder Type	Fahrenheit	Celsius
Easy	1325°	711°
Medium	1390°	747°
Hard	1425°	773°
Eutectic	1460°	793°
IT	1490°	809°

RACHEL DOW is a studio artist specializing in fabricated sterling silver, metal clay, and found object jewelry. She has received a B.A. in photography, and her M.A. in art education comes from California State University at Northridge. She has a certification in metal clay, and also received formal training in jewelry fabrication from the Metals Edge Studio in Scottsdale, Arizona. Dow's work is shown in selected galleries and studios. www.rmddesigns.com

JOANNA GOLLBERG is a studio artist working in Asheville, North Carolina. She graduated from the Fashion Institute of Technology with a degree in jewelry design, and exhibits her work at craft fairs and galleries throughout the United States. Gollberg is the author of two books, *Making Metal Jewelry* (Lark Books, 2003) and *Creative Metal Crafts* (Lark Books, 2004).

ELIZABETH A. HAKE discovered the passion of her life in 1993 during her first jewelry class. In 1996 she received a B.F.A. in metalsmithing and jewelry from Northern Michigan University. She recently spent a year as an artist-in-residence at Arrowmont School in Gatlinburg, Tennessee, then returned to her home in western North Carolina, where she continues to pursue a career as a visual artist and teacher. Hake primarily uses rubber and silver, combining the two materials to create one-of-a-kind work as well as a line of production pieces.

MARY HETTMANSPERGER is an award-winning fiber artist who focuses on basketry, metals, and beadwork. Inspired by things that grow and evolve, she uses each piece as a foundation for the next, avoiding replication and improving upon the strengths of a piece. Hettmansperger has taught for 21 years. She exhibits at galleries and art shows and has had her work published in *Fiberarts Design Book 7*.

JASON JANOW is a jewelry designer and metalsmith based in Asheville, North Carolina. A graduate of Haywood Community College, Janow is a member of the Society of North American Goldsmiths and the American Art Council. Recent exhibitions include the Southern Highlands Craft Guild Show and "The Ne(X)t Generation of Jewelry" at the Grovewood Gallery in Asheville.

SUSAN LENART KAZMER is a studio artist and award-winning jewelry designer whose work has sold in galleries around the globe. Kazmer's recent creations—a combination of game pieces, found objects, and crafted elements—have been exhibited in a number of museums, among them the Art Institute in New York. Numerous books and publications, including *Lapidary Journal* and *Bead and Button*, have reproduced her work. She has taught workshops on metalwork, such as "Altered Surface on Metal" and "Objects and Elements in Jewelry," at Baum School of Art, Brookfield Craft Center, and other art schools. www.susanlenartkazmer.net

contributing artists (continued)

BRENDA SUE LANSDOWNE still owns her first creation: a 1988 confection of old moiré fabric, lace, and Victorian gold-filled bar pins. She has since sold thousands of her pieces.

In 1993 she opened B'sue Boutiques, a company of seven artisans making found item, charm, and button jewelry for the gift market. Landsdowne's current website boasts more than 1,600 products, including her own work, select vintage jewelry, her favorite chains and stones, and unique, rare, and hard-to-find jewelry components. It also offers advice on sorting old jewelry for value, and tips on making collage jewelry, hatpins, charm bracelets, and more. www.bsueboutiques.com

LILLA LE VINE grew up on a remote sheep station in New Zealand. As a fiber artist who likes to explore all forms of creativity, her latest projects include ribbon and machine stitchery, fabric and paper collage, ephemera crafts, altered books, and anything else she dreams up.

Now a resident of Hawaii, Le Vine is a sought-after teacher, and a member of the Fiber Arts Guild, a stamp club, and an altered book group. She sells her designs on several web sites and creates projects for magazines in the United States and Australia.

BRAXTON MORRIS finds creative satisfaction in re-purposing objects. She makes decorative artwork for the home and unconventional accessories to wear.

MERRY RADTKE is a studio metal artist and art teacher residing in Orchard Park, New York. She has exhibited in galleries, exhibitions, and shows across the United States. Radtke taught three-dimensional design and jewelry at the college level for five years. She now teaches high school art, gives private studio lessons, and offers various workshops in creative metals for children and adults. Radtke holds a masters degree in art education from the Rochester Institute of Technology, and a B.F.A. from the State University of New York College at Buffalo where she majored in jewelry design.

KRISTIN MITSU SHIGA grew up in New York City with a strong sense of identity, a curiosity for intricate objects, and a love for the foods and languages of many cultures. She attended Syracuse University for six years, where she got her first taste of metalsmithing.

Mitsu Shiga worked as a bench jeweler for a designer, then opened her own business. After developing a metalsmithing program at an adult education center, she discovered her other passion: teaching. She has exhibited nationally since 1993, and her work appears in several books and publications.

KATHY STOFFEL'S range of interests includes creating faux finishes on furniture, sewing, quilting, mosaics, decoupage, and jewelry. She learned to appreciate antiques and collectibles while attending flea markets, auctions, and antique shows.

Designing jewelry incorporating found objects compels her because it combines an old love of collecting with her new passion for beads. She finds it delightful to see an everyday object used in unexpected ways. For Stoffel, adornments made from the objects of daily life link us to ancient roots.

Her jewelry appears on www.eclecticbeadery.com, under the logo M&G's Treasures.

TERRY TAYLOR'S creative work takes many forms: from jewelry to mixed-media pieces to craft-projects-on-demand for Lark Books. He has studied jewelry and metalwork at John C. Campbell Folk School, Appalachian Center for Crafts, and Haystack Mountain School of Crafts.

GAE WEBSTER is a mixed-media artist whose works reflect organic textures and shapes. Webster exhibits in solo shows, has completed many commissioned works, and her work appears in collections around the world. She currently tutors in jewelry, abstract painting, and book art.

For her jewelry, Webster likes to recreate or mount often-familiar objects, perhaps from the sea or garden, in precious metals. She then combines them to tell stories or recall special universal memories.

Webster lives in Auckland, New Zealand, and is married to a deliciously understanding man; she has three wonderful adult children and a very large dog named Boadicea. View other art pieces at www.artsmith.co.nz

JANE ANN WYNN creates jewelry, mixed-media artworks, assemblages, collages, sculpture, digital art, and fiber pieces. She has a B.F.A. in studio art from the University of Maryland, and an M.F.A. in inter-related media from Towson University.

"Every object is created with its own specific purpose in life. Then I find it, knock it to the ground and build it back up again!" she states.

As she creates mixed-media sculptural pieces, she works in an intuitive manner. Whether Wynn finds the object, or it finds her, she assembles a personal narrative, creating an odd mixture of the past and present.

gallery artist index/acknowledgments

Thanks to the talented and industrious staff at Lark Books who helped produce this book, especially Nathalie Mornu, Terry Taylor, Nicole Tuggle, and Tom Metcalf. Thanks to the contributing artists for sharing their creative abilities, imaginative designs, and technical assistance. Thanks to Robert W. Ebendorf. Thanks to the art galleries, organizations, schools, and publications that passionately support, promote, and advance the field of found object jewelry. Thanks to Sara Le Van, who taught me to see.

EMIKO OYE
Showroom 007 and *Pioneer a Movement*, from the *Patent Pending Collection*, 1999
Left, 3½ in. (8.9 cm) in diameter; right, 4 in. (10.2 cm) in diameter
Recycled plastic price tags, recycled plastic film, recycled rubber, sterling silver, steel
Photo by Don Felton

index

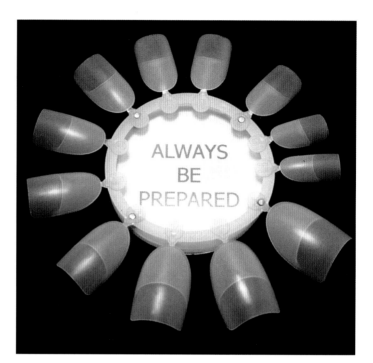

LESLIE A. SCHUG
Always Be Prepared, 2000
2⅞ x 3/8 in. (7.3 x 1 cm)
Silver, plastic, paper, copper
Photo by K. Browne

NOTES ABOUT SUPPLIERS

Usually, the supplies you need for making the projects in Lark books can be found at your local craft supply store, discount mart, home improvement center, or retail shop relevant to the topic of the book. Occasionally, however, you may need to buy materials or tools from specialty suppliers. In order to provide you with the most up-to-date information, we have created a listing of suppliers on our Web site, which we update on a regular basis. Visit us at www.larkbooks.com, click on "Craft Supply Sources," and then click on the relevant topic. You will find numerous companies listed with their web address and/or mailing address and phone number.